Life Skills for High School Teens:Thriving in Transition

A Teen's Guide to Strategies for Stress Reduction,Substance Abuse Prevention,Your Safe Digital Footprint, and so much more

Robert James Ryan

Contents

Introduction

In today's world, teenagers face more intense and complex pressures than ever before. A staggering 70% report feeling overwhelmed by the daily challenges. This statistic highlights the urgent need for support and sets the stage for a transformative journey we will undertake together. "Life Skills for High School Teens: Thriving in Transition" is not just a book; it's a lifeline designed to empower you, the high school teens, and your parents to navigate the intricate transition to adulthood with skill, understanding, and confidence.

My vision for this book is clear: to equip you with an arsenal of life skills crucial for overcoming the myriad of challenges that come your way. This guide covers everything from mastering effective communication to reducing stress, helping to prevent substance abuse, and navigating the complex dynamics of friendships and peer pressure. But it doesn't stop there. Understanding the importance of digital safety, financial literacy, and mental health is critical to your journey toward a balanced and fulfilling life.

As the author of this comprehensive guide, my passion for helping teens and their parents through these critical years is deeply personal. Drawing from my experiences raising three teenagers and backed by the latest research, I've dedicated myself to creating an informative, empathetic, and engaging resource. My journey has taught me that your challenges are unique, but overcoming them is entirely possible with the right tools and support.

This book is meticulously crafted for you—the 13—to 19-year-old teenagers and your parents. It aims to bridge the gap between you and your parents or guardians, fostering an environment of mutual understanding, respect, and support. Through real-life scenarios, actionable tips, and exercises, you'll find practical advice that can be seamlessly integrated into your daily lives.

In today's world, teenagers face more intense and complex pressures than ever before. "Life Skills for High School Teens: "Thriving in Transition" stands out because it doesn't just address the issues. It delves into the heart of each challenge, offering innovative and practical strategies.

As we embark on this path together, I want you to feel understood, supported, and hopeful. The challenges of high school and the transition to adulthood are real, but so is your potential to navigate them successfully. With an open mind and a willingness to learn and grow, there's no limit to what you can achieve.

So, I invite you to turn the page and join me in exploring the comprehensive, engaging, and transformative world of "Life Skills for High School Teens: Thriving in Transition." Together, we can face the challenges, embrace the opportunities, and emerge stronger on the other side. The secret here is to make this fun and entertaining. Don't try to do too much all at once. Read a chapter

or two and let it sink in. Maybe take a break and then coi later. The important thing is to learn at your own pace these tips to help you wherever you may be.

Thank you for taking the time to read this. I sincerel helps you in your day-to-day life and inspires you to help well

Chapter One

Facing Social Challenges

Imagine walking down a hallway, your footsteps echoing against the lockers - a familiar scene, right? Now, picture the whispers that sometimes follow, the pointed fingers, and the screens lighting up with anything but friendly messages. These aren't scenes from a movie but the harsh realities of bullying. It's not just about the physical confrontations; spoken and typed words carry weight, often leaving scars deeper than any physical wound could. This chapter isn't just about understanding bullying; it's about flipping the script. It's about empowerment, assertiveness, and the collective power of empathy to change the narrative.

Recognizing Bullying. Bullying isn't just about the big kid in the playground demanding lunch money. It's evolved, taking on forms that can be harder to recognize but just as damaging. There's verbal bullying, where words cut deep, and social bullying, where rumors and exclusion can make school feel like a prison. And then there's cyberbullying, where texts and online posts become weapons. Recognizing bullying is the first step to stopping it. It's about seeing the signs, not just in your own experiences but in those around you. When laughter comes at someone else's expense or online jokes get personal, it's more than just fun and games; it's bullying.

Empowerment and Assertiveness. Standing up to bullies isn't about matching their aggression with your own. It's about assertiveness, the strength to voice your resistance without stepping over the line. Picture this: someone throws a hurtful comment your way, and instead of letting it slide or firing back with anger, you stand your ground. You tell them, calmly and clearly, that what they're doing isn't okay. It's not about confrontation but about setting boundaries. It's about showing that their words don't define you. And when you do this, you're not just standing up for yourself but setting an example for others.

Seeking Support. No one should face bullying alone. It's like trying to lift a boulder when all you need to do is ask for help, and suddenly, it's manageable. Seeking support means turning to friends who have your back, adults who can intervene, and authorities who can take action. It's about knowing who to turn to and how to ask for help. Schools often have counselors trained for these situations, and many communities offer resources specifically designed to combat bullying. Remember, asking for help isn't a sign of weakness; it's a strategic move towards a solution.

Fostering Empathy. Imagine a school where empathy outweighs apathy, where bystanders become upstanders. Fostering empathy is about creating an environment where everyone looks out for each other. It's about understanding that the bullied person could just as quickly be you or someone you care about. When you see someone being bullied, don't just walk by. Offer them support, report what you saw, or stand by their side. Sometimes, knowing they're not alone is enough to give someone the strength to face another day.

Facing social challenges like bullying requires courage, but it's not a battle you have to fight alone. It's about recognizing the problem, standing up for yourself and others, seeking support, and fostering an environment where empathy drowns out hate. It's about changing the narrative, one act of courage at a time.

Having access to a wide range of resources can be incredibly empowering for those affected by bullying. Below is a comprehensive list that includes hotlines, websites, and suggestions for local organizations. It also includes journaling prompts for self-reflection and strategies to foster resilience and empathy. This toolkit aims to offer immediate support and encourage long-term healing and community building.

Hotlines

1. **StopBullying.gov**

- Website: https://www.stopbullying.gov

- Information on prevention and response to bullying, including cyberbullying.

1. **Kids Help Phone (Canada)**

- Call: 1-800-668-6868

- Text: CONNECT to 686868

- Website: https://kidshelpphone.ca/

1. **Childline (UK)**

- Call: 0800 1111

- Website: https://www.childline.org.uk/

1. **Bullying UK**

2. Helpline: 0808 800 2222

- Website: https://www.bullying.co.uk/

Websites
1. **Bullying No Way! (Australia)**

- Website: https://bullyingnoway.gov.au/

1. **Cyberbully Help**

- Website: http://www.cyberbullyhelp.com

1. **The Trevor Project**

- Website: https://www.thetrevorproject.org/

1. **STOMP Out Bullying**

- Website: https://www.stompoutbullying.org

1. **PACER's National Bullying Prevention Center**

- Website:https://www.pacer.org/bullying

Local Organizations. Seek local community centers, schools, and mental health organizations for workshops, support groups, and counseling addressing bullying.

Journaling Prompts for Self-Reflection

1. Reflect on a time you felt bullied or witnessed bullying. How did it affect you emotionally?

2. Consider your strengths that could help you or others stand against bullying.

3. Write a letter of advice to someone younger experiencing bullying, sharing wisdom from your own experiences.

Strategies for Building Assertiveness

- Practice assertive communication, focusing on expressing your needs and boundaries clearly and respectfully.

- Engage in role-playing exercises to build confidence in handling confrontational situations.

Tips for Fostering an Empathetic Community

- Lead with empathy and kindness in all interactions, setting a positive example for others.

- Encourage open discussions about emotions, bullying experiences, and the importance of mutual support.

Navigating Peer Pressure: How to Make Your Own Choices. Peer pressure is like a tide; sometimes, it's barely noticeable, gently nudging you along, and at other times, it's a mighty wave, threatening to sweep you off your feet and carry you away from your true self. The force exerted by friends, classmates, or social circles compels you to act in a certain way, to fit in, or to be part of the group. This invisible force can shape decisions, influence behavior, and sometimes lead to regrettable choices. But remember, every tide can be navigated with skill and patience.

Understanding Peer Pressure. It operates subtly, often masked as friendly suggestions or harmless fun. The mechanics are simple yet profound: it leverages our innate desire for belonging and acceptance, making resisting challenging. It's crucial to recognize its presence in daily scenarios, whether it's a nudge to skip class, a push towards trying something risky, or the expectation to conform to specific group norms. Remember, recognizing peer pressure is the first step in navigating it.

Staying True to Oneself. The essence of resisting peer pressure lies in the core belief of staying true to oneself. It's about knowing who you are, what you stand for, and where your boundaries lie. Here's how to maintain your integrity amidst the push and pull of peer influences:

- Reflect regularly on your values and beliefs. What's important to you? What won't you compromise on?

- Practice saying no in lower-stakes situations to build your confidence.

- Visualize scenarios where you might face peer pressure and mentally rehearse your response.

Maintaining your identity when the current tries to carry you away requires a strong anchor. Your values and beliefs anchor you, keeping you grounded even in the face of strong tides.

Assertiveness Skills. Assertiveness is the rudder that helps you navigate the waters of peer pressure. It's the ability to express your thoughts, feelings, and beliefs openly, honestly, and directly without infringing on the rights of others. Here are some strategies to enhance your assertiveness:

- Use "I" statements to express how you feel about a situation without placing blame. For example, "I feel uncomfortable when we talk about skipping class."

- Practice a firm yet polite tone. Your voice should convey confidence, not aggression.

- Rehearse your responses. Preparing a clear, concise reply can make all the difference when the moment arrives.

Being assertive doesn't mean being inflexible. It's about communicating your stance in a way that respects yourself and others.

Finding Supportive Peers. The voyage becomes less daunting when you have the right crew. Surrounding yourself with peers who respect and support your choices can turn the stormy seas of peer pressure into navigable waters. Here's how to find and cultivate these relationships:

- Look for friends who share your interests and values. Clubs, teams, and groups centered around common goals can be great starting points.

- Pay attention to how potential friends react to differences in opinion. Do they respect differing views, or do they pressure others to conform?

- Be that friend who supports others in their choices. Kindness and respect are contagious.

Ultimately, the circles we choose to be part of significantly impact our ability to stand firm in the face of peer pressure. Opting for a supportive, respectful group bolsters our resilience and enriches our journey with meaningful relationships.

Navigating peer pressure is an art, one that involves recognizing its presence, staying anchored in your values, steering confidently with assertiveness, and choosing suitable companions for your journey. It's about making choices that reflect your true self, unaffected by the tides of conformity and expectation. Every decision aligned with your values is a step toward a more authentic and fulfilling life.

The Role of Social Media in Friendships: The Good, The Bad, and The Ugly. In an age where our digital footprints span wider than ever, social media has become the town square of modern friendships. It allows us to cross time zones and distances with a simple click, making it easier to stay woven into each other's lives. But as with any bustling square, it's not without its shadows.

Connecting and Reconnecting. Social media platforms serve as bridges, linking us to friends from different chapters of our lives. Remember the friend who moved away in third grade? Or the group you met at summer camp? Social media rekindles these connections, transforming "what ifs" into "remember whens." It's like having a reunion at your fingertips, where memories are shared and new ones are created. This digital connectivity ensures that we can still be part of each other's journey no matter where life takes us.

- **Friend Suggestions**: Utilize features like "People You May Know" to find old friends and acquaintances.

- **Memory Features**: Share and reminisce over memories that social media platforms often remind you of.

- **Group Chats/Groups**: Create or join groups dedicated to specific interests or shared experiences to strengthen bonds.

Misunderstandings and Conflicts. However, the ease of communication that social media offers can sometimes be its downfall. Misunderstandings flourish where tone and context are lost in translation. A joke might come off as a jab; a comment might seem colder than intended. These digital misinterpretations can escalate, straining friendships. When conflicts arise:

- **Take it Offline**: Resolve misunderstandings face-to-face or over a call. Tone and intent are more precise, reducing the likelihood of further miscommunication.

- **Pause Before You Post**: If a friend's post or comment upsets you, take a moment to cool down before responding.

- **Clarify Intentions**: If a message or post is ambiguous, ask for clarification. Often, conflicts stem from simple misunderstandings rather than actual disputes.

Social Media Pressure. Amidst the glossy pictures and curated posts, social media crafts an illusion of perfection. It's easy to fall into the trap of comparing your behind-the-scenes with everyone else's highlight reel. This pressure to present a flawless life can strain friendships, as authenticity takes a back seat to appearances. To combat this:

- **Celebrate Authenticity**: Post content that reflects your real life, not just the polished parts. Embrace and encourage authenticity.

- **Limit Comparison**: Remember that social media is a curated snapshot, not the whole picture. Focus on your journey, not how it compares to others.

- **Curate Your Feed**: Follow accounts that uplift and inspire you. If certain content fuels comparison or discontent, unfollow it.

Healthy Social Media Habits

To ensure that social media remains a tool for connection rather than a wedge driving friends apart, consider adopting these healthy habits:

- **Digital Detoxes**: Regularly unplug from social media to reconnect with the world around you. This will refresh your perspective and recharge your appreciation for direct human connections.

- **Be Intentional**: Use social media with purpose, whether staying informed, sharing passions, or keeping in touch with friends. Avoid mindless scrolling.

- **Supportive Interactions**: Engage with friends' posts in meaningful ways. Leave thoughtful comments, share uplifting content, and use direct messaging for more personal conversations.

- **Set Boundaries**: Be mindful of your time on social media. Set specific times for checking platforms and stick to them to prevent them from overshadowing face-to-face interactions.

Social media threads run bright and dark in weaving the fabric of modern friendships. With awareness and intention, it can enrich connections and easily bridge distances and differences. Yet, it demands a balance, a conscious effort to ensure that the heart of friendship remains genuine, supportive, and authentic beneath the digital avatars and screens. As we navigate this digital age, let's use social media to connect with friends and nurture those connections, making them stronger, deeper, and more meaningful.

Finding Your Crowd: The Importance of Community and Belonging. Discovering a community that resonates with your spirit and interests isn't just about adding social engagements to your calendar. It's a deeper dive into aligning your passions with groups that share those same flames of interest. Whether it's the guitar strum that calls to you or the quiet hum of a computer running code, there's a group out there waiting for you to join the chorus.

Exploring Interests. Diving into personal hobbies and passions is more than a solitary journey; it's a beacon for finding your tribe. Imagine turning a corner in exploring medieval literature

and finding a weekly group meeting to discuss the tales that ig-
nite your imagination. In your quest to perfect your three-point-
er on the basketball court, you stumble upon a community
league. These aren't just coincidences; they're the universe guiding you towards your people. To find these connections:

- Start with local community boards or social media
  groups dedicated to your interest.

- Visit local events or workshops that cater to your hobby.
  You'll polish your skills and meet others who share your
  enthusiasm.

- Feel free to initiate a new group if one doesn't exist.
  Sometimes, the crowd finds you when you light the
  beacon.

Community Involvement. Engaging in community service
or joining clubs isn't just an act of benevolence or a resume
builder. It's a fertile ground for nurturing relationships with
those who share your values. Whether cleaning up local parks
or advocating for community issues, giving back creates a bond
beyond the surface level. Consider:

- Volunteering for causes you're passionate about. Not
  only do you contribute to meaningful change, but you
  also meet others with a similar drive.

- Joining clubs or groups within your school or community. These structured settings provide a steady platform for relationships to bloom over shared goals.

Remember, it's not just about what you're doing together; it's about the shared purpose that ties you all.

The Value of Diversity. In the tapestry of humanity, every thread is unique, contributing to the beauty of the whole. Embracing diversity in your community and friendships enriches your perspective, opening you to experiences and viewpoints beyond your own. Imagine sitting at a table where every person comes from a different background, each sharing stories that paint a picture of a world much more extensive than your own. This is where growth happens. To cultivate this diversity:

- Actively seek out groups and individuals with varying experiences and backgrounds. The richness of their stories adds depth to your understanding of the world.

- Listen with an open heart and mind. Sometimes, understanding comes not from speaking but from genuinely hearing what others say.

- Challenge your assumptions and biases. Growth is often found in uncomfortable spaces where we confront what we thought we knew.

In diversity, there's a harmony that resonates with the truth of our shared humanity, reminding us that we're all part of a larger community.

Creating Inclusive Spaces. Imagine a garden where every plant, regardless of origin, is nurtured to bloom. This is the essence of creating inclusive spaces - environments where everyone feels valued and heard regardless of background. It's not just about opening the door; it's about welcoming everyone into the room. Here's how you can foster such spaces:

- Practice active listening and ensure everyone has a chance to speak. Inclusivity starts with making sure all voices are heard.

- Be mindful of language and actions that might inadvertently exclude or offend. Subtle signals often speak the loudest.

- Educate yourself and others about inclusivity. It's a journey of learning, unlearning, and relearning.

- Advocate for inclusive practices in your clubs, groups, and community. Change often starts with a single voice daring to speak up.

Consider how every interaction and decision creates a space where everyone feels they belong. True community thrives in these environments, built on the foundational pillars of respect, understanding, and mutual support.

As you wade through the waters of finding where you belong, remember that it's not just about fitting into a pre-existing mold. It's about discovering spaces where your unique self is accepted and celebrated. In these communities, we find friends and a sense of home.

Transitioning to College: Maintaining Old Friendships While Building New Ones

Moving to college marks a significant phase in life, filled with excitement and, undeniably, a bit of apprehension. It's a time when the comfort of familiar faces gives way to the prospect of meeting new ones. How do you keep the connections that have been your anchor while allowing room for new ones that could unexpectedly enrich your life?

Keeping in Touch. Staying connected with high school friends doesn't have to be a casualty of your college transition. Modern technology offers countless ways to maintain these relationships despite being miles apart.

- **Scheduled Video Calls**: Set up regular video chats. This could be as structured as a monthly catch-up or as spontaneous as a quick call to share a funny incident.

- **Social Media**: Use social platforms for updates and engaging with your friends' lives. Comment on their achievements and challenges.

- **Visit Plans**: Whenever possible, plan visits. These don't always have to be grand reunions; sometimes, a quick coffee catch-up during breaks can keep the friendship spark alive.

The trick lies in being intentional. Remember, it's about the quality of connections, not the quantity.

Openness to New Relationships. Entering college is akin to stepping into a broader horizon. Here, you'll encounter people with unique stories and perspectives from various backgrounds.

- **Join** clubs or societies that align with your interests. This is a natural setting to meet like-minded individuals.

- **Study Groups**: Form or join study groups. These can ease academic pressures while fostering new friendships.

- **Be Approachable**: Sometimes, a smile or a simple hello can open the door to a conversation and, possibly, a lasting friendship.

Embrace the diversity of people you meet. Each new connection offers a window into different worlds and experiences.

Balancing Old and New. Juggling existing friendships while nurturing new ones is akin to walking a tightrope; it requires balance, focus, and a bit of grace.

- **Open Communication**: Be honest with your old friends about your new life and make them feel they're still a significant part of it.

- **Inclusivity**: When possible, introduce your old friends to your new ones. Merging different circles can lead to enriched experiences for everyone involved.

- **Prioritize**: There will be times when you must choose where to invest your time and energy. Make these choices based on who needs you more now, without completely neglecting the other.

It's about finding harmony between the old and the new, ensuring that neither is left in the shadows.

Navigating Changes. Friendships, like individuals, evolve. College life, with its myriad of experiences, accelerates this evolution.

- **Accept Change**: Some friendships might naturally fade

while others grow stronger. It's a normal part of life's ebb and flow.

- **Honest Conversations**: A heartfelt conversation can sometimes bridge the gap if a friendship drifts. Other times, it might bring closure.

- **Cherish Memories**: Regardless of how friendships transform, cherish the memories and lessons they've provided. Every friendship leaves a mark, shaping you into who you are.

Navigating these changes requires a blend of acceptance, communication, and appreciation. Though bittersweet, it's a journey that leads to personal growth and a deeper understanding of relationships.

In wrapping up, the transition to college presents an exciting opportunity to widen your social circle while keeping the bonds that have supported you thus far. It's a delicate dance of staying connected with your past and being open to the future. As you move forward, remember that every friendship, old or new, is a chapter in the story of your life. Each contributes to your journey, offering lessons, laughter, and a sense of belonging.

As we transition from focusing on friendships and social dynamics to understanding personal identity and self-expression, these elements are crucial as they form the foundation for building and maintaining our relationships.

Chapter Two
Mental Health Matters

Picture yourself standing at the edge of a vast ocean, staring into the horizon where the sky meets the water. The ocean's surface is sometimes calm, reflecting the sun's warm glow, and at other times, it's tumultuous, with waves crashing and churning. This ocean is like our mental health: ever-changing, deeply powerful, and deserving of attention and respect. In this chapter, we focus on navigating through the rough waters of anxiety and depression, ensuring you have the right tools and knowledge to keep your boat steady, even in the stormiest weather.

Recognizing Symptoms. Anxiety and depression are not just bad moods or phases; they're natural, often debilitating conditions that affect millions. But how can you tell if what you're experiencing is more than just a rough patch? Some signs to watch out for include:

- **Persistent Sadness or Worry**: Feeling down or anxious

more days than not.

- **Changes in Sleep Patterns**: Sleeping too much or too little.

- **Loss of Interest**: Not enjoying activities you used to love.

- **Energy Drain**: Feeling tired all the time without a physical reason.

- **Concentration Trouble**: Difficulty focusing on tasks or making decisions.

- **Appetite Changes**: Eating much more or much less than usual.

- **Irritability**: Getting annoyed easily.

- **Unexplained Aches**: Experiencing headaches, stomachaches, or other pains without a clear cause.

If these feel familiar, know you're not alone. Recognizing these signs is the first step toward getting the help you need.

Seeking Professional Help. Reaching out for help can feel daunting, but it's a brave and necessary step. Start with a trusted adult—a family member, teacher, or school counselor—who can guide you to the right resources. Many schools offer confidential counseling services; some clinics specialize in teen mental health. Remember, seeking help is a sign of strength, not weakness. It's about taking control of your well-being.

When you're ready to see a professional, here are a few tips:

- **Prepare for the Appointment**: Write down what you've been feeling and experiencing, no matter how small it seems.

- **Be Open and Honest**: The more your therapist or counselor knows, the better they can help you.

- **Ask Questions**: If you need clarification on something, ask. This is your journey, and understanding each step is crucial.

Self-Help Strategies. While professional support is critical, there are also strategies you can use to manage mild symptoms of anxiety and depression on your own:

- **Physical Activity**: Exercise releases endorphins, which can boost your mood. Even a short walk can make a difference.

- **Mindfulness and Meditation**: These practices can help you stay present and reduce feelings of anxiety.

- **Healthy Routines**: Try to maintain a regular sleep schedule, eat balanced meals, and engage in enjoyable activities.

- **Journaling**: Writing down your thoughts and feelings can be a robust process.

Remember, these aren't replacements for professional help, but they can be part of a comprehensive approach to managing your mental health.

De-stigmatizing Mental Health Issues. For too long, mental health issues have been wrapped in stigma, making it harder for those struggling to speak out and seek help. It's time to change the narrative. Mental health is just as important as physical health, and acknowledging that is the first step toward creating a more understanding and supportive society.

Here are ways we can all contribute to de-stigmatizing mental health:

- **Educate Yourself and Others**: Learn about mental health issues and share your knowledge. The more we know, the less we fear.

- **Be Mindful of Language**: Words matter. Avoid using terms like "crazy" or "psycho" to describe someone.

- **Listen Without Judgment**: If someone opens up to you about their struggles, listen with empathy and without making assumptions.

- **Share Your Story**: If you're comfortable, sharing your experiences can help others feel less alone and encourage them to seek help.

Here's a curated list encompassing hotlines, websites, and apps designed to provide support, information, and immediate assistance for teenagers navigating mental health challenges. This list is intended as a starting point, and I encourage further exploration and consultation with healthcare professionals for personalized advice.

Hotlines

1. **National Suicide Prevention Lifeline (U.S.)**: Available 24/7 for anyone in suicidal crisis or emotional distress. Call 1-800-273-TALK (1-800-273-8255).

2. **Crisis Text Line (U.S. & Canada)**: Text HOME to 741741 (U.S.) or 686868 (Canada) for 24/7 support from trained crisis counselors.

3. **Kids Help Phone (Canada)**: Offers 24/7 counseling and information services for young people. Call 1-800-668-6868 or text CONNECT to 686868.

4. **Childline (UK)**: This is for children and teens under 19 and offers confidential support with any issue. Call 0800 1111.

5. **Lifeline (Australia)**: This organization provides 24/7 crisis support and suicide prevention services. Call 13 11 14.

Websites

1. **Teen Mental Health**: Provides scientifically reliable information about teen mental health and mental disorders. https://mentalhealthliteracy.org/

2. **The Trevor Project**: Offers crisis intervention and suicide prevention services to LGBTQ young people under 25. https://www.thetrevorproject.org/

3. **Mind (UK)**: Provides advice and support to anyone experiencing a mental health problem. https://www.mind

.org.uk/

4. **Headspace (Australia)**: Offers support, information, and advice for young people experiencing difficulties with mental health. https://headspace.org.au/

5. **YoungMinds (UK)**: A charity fighting for children and young people's mental health, offering support and resources. https://www.youngminds.org.uk/

Apps

1. **Headspace**: An app offering guided meditation sessions and mindfulness training to reduce stress and improve wellbeing.

2. **Calm**: This site provides meditation techniques, sleep stories, and relaxation tools to help lower stress and improve sleep quality.

3. **Moodfit** is a tool to help you track and improve your mood, offering resources to understand and improve mental health.

4. **Talkspace** is an online therapy service that connects users with licensed therapists for text, audio, and video sessions.

5. **Woebot**: An AI-powered chatbot designed to help users manage their emotions and mental health through therapeutic conversations.

Remember, these resources can provide immediate support and valuable information, but they do not replace professional medical advice. It's crucial to seek a healthcare provider for personalized guidance and support tailored to individual needs.

Navigating the complexities of mental health can feel like sailing through a vast, unpredictable ocean. But with the proper support, tools, and knowledge, you can learn to steer your ship through even the most challenging waters, finding calm and clarity. Remember, it's okay to ask for help and not to be okay. You're not alone, and there's a whole community ready to support you on your path to well-being.

The Importance of Self-Care: Tips for Teens. In today's fast-paced world, where every moment seems accounted for—from school deadlines to part-time jobs and social obligations—the idea of dedicating time to oneself might feel like a luxury we can't afford. Yet, self-care is far from a mere indulgence. Maintaining balance is critical, ensuring our mental, emotional, and physical tanks are sufficiently fueled to navigate life's demands. It's about giving ourselves permission to pause, breathe, and attend to our needs, understanding that this, in turn, enhances our capacity to meet our responsibilities and care for others.

Defining Self-Care. Self-care encompasses any activity we do deliberately to take care of our mental, emotional, and physical health. Contrary to what social media might portray, it's not all bubble baths and spa days. It's a broad spectrum that includes the basics like adequate sleep, balanced nutrition, and physical activity, but it also extends to setting boundaries, pursuing hobbies, and practicing mindfulness. The essence of self-care lies in being mindful of our own needs, listening to our bodies and minds, and taking steps to meet those needs.

Practical Self-Care Activities. Self-care looks different for everyone. What soothes one person might not work for another, and that's perfectly fine. Here's a variety of activities that might resonate with different preferences:

- **Creative Outlets**: Drawing, painting, writing, or playing an instrument can be therapeutic ways to express feelings and relieve stress.

- **Physical Activity**: Whether it's a structured workout, a dance session in your room, or a walk in the park, moving your body releases tension and boosts mood.

- **Tech Break**: Periodically unplugging from digital devices can reduce information overload and give your mind a much-needed break.

- **Mindful Eating**: Paying attention to what and how you eat can improve your relationship with food and body image.

- **Quality Time**: Spending time with friends or family who uplift you, or even quality time alone, can recharge your emotional batteries.

Balancing Self-Care with Responsibilities. Finding time for self-care amidst a packed schedule is challenging but not impossible. Here are strategies to integrate self-care into your daily life:

- **Schedule It**: Treat self-care like any other important activity—block off time in your calendar.

- **Combine Activities**: Listen to a podcast or an audiobook while exercising or doing chores.

- **Set Boundaries**: If you are already stretched thin, learn to avoid additional responsibilities. Protecting your time is a form of self-care.

- **Use Downtime Wisely**: Short breaks between tasks can be opportunities for quick self-care, like stretching, deep breathing, or savoring a cup of tea.

Self-Care and Self-Compassion. Self-compassion is at the heart of self-care—treating yourself with the same kindness, concern, and support you'd offer a good friend. It's about acknowledging our struggles, accepting our imperfections, and being gentle with ourselves in the face of challenges. Self-compassion reminds us that we're not alone in our struggles and encourages an attitude of care rather than criticism.

- **Self-Talk**: Pay attention to how you talk to yourself. Replace self-criticism with supportive and understanding language.

- **Forgive Yourself**: Mistakes are part of being human. Forgive yourself and view setbacks as opportunities to learn.

- **Celebrate Wins**: Acknowledge and celebrate your achievements, no matter how small. Recognizing your efforts fosters a positive self-view.

Building a Support System: Finding and Offering Help. Navigating the ups and downs of teenage years can feel like steering a ship through uncharted waters. Sometimes, the seas are calm, and at other times, they're stormy and unpredictable. A reliable support system can make all the difference during those turbulent times. It's like having a lighthouse guiding you safely to shore.

Identifying Support Networks. A strong support network isn't just about having people around; it's about having the right people around—those who genuinely care about your well-being and are there for you, rain or shine. Here's how to spot and build your crew:

- **Family Members**: Often, the family can be your first line of support. They know you well and are vested in your happiness and success.

- **Friends Who Truly Get You**: Look for friends who listen without judgment, offer encouragement, and respect your feelings and boundaries.

- **Teachers and School Counselors**: These professionals can provide guidance, listen sympathetically, and connect you with additional resources.

- **Online Communities**: If you're struggling to find support in your immediate environment, online forums and social media groups can offer solidarity and understanding from those with similar experiences.

Building this network takes time and effort, but the foundation of trust and mutual respect it's built on is invaluable. Being a Supportive Friend: Just as you look for support, be ready to extend it. Helping a friend through a tough time strengthens your relationship and can be incredibly rewarding. Here are some ways to be the friend someone can lean on:

- **Listen More Than You Speak**: Sometimes, someone needs to be heard. Resist the urge to offer quick fixes and be present.

- **Encourage Professional Help When Needed**: Recognize when a friend's needs exceed what you can provide and encourage them to seek help from a mental health professional.

- **Check-In Regularly**: A simple message asking how they're doing can mean the world to someone struggling.

- **Educate Yourself**: Understanding more about what your friend is going through can help you provide better support.

Remember, being a supportive friend also means caring for your mental health. You can't pour from an empty cup.

Community and Online Resources. Sometimes, your support might not be available in your immediate circle. That's where community and online resources come into play. They can offer specialized assistance and a sense of belonging that's hard to find elsewhere. Consider these options:

- **Mental Health Organizations**: Many organizations offer hotlines, counseling services, and educational materials that can be invaluable resources.

- **Support Groups**: In-person and online support groups bring together people facing similar challenges, providing a platform to share experiences and coping strategies.

- **Educational Websites and Apps**: Websites and apps dedicated to mental health education can offer insights and tools for managing your well-being.

Exploring these resources might introduce you to new coping mechanisms and perspectives, enriching your support system.

The Power of Peer Support. Peer support groups, whether found in school, local community centers, or online, offer a unique form of empathy and understanding. Engaging with peers who have walked a similar path can be incredibly validating and empowering. Here's what makes peer support so unique:

- **Mutual Understanding**: There's comfort in knowing you're not alone in your experiences. Peer support groups provide a safe space to share and learn from each other.

- **Shared Growth**: A collective sense of progress and achievement can boost everyone's morale as you navigate your challenges together.

- **Empowerment**: Being part of a group that encourages taking control of one's mental health can be a powerful motivator.

While peer support groups are a fantastic resource, it's important to remember they complement, rather than replace, professional mental health services. They're part of a broader strategy for maintaining mental health and well-being.

Building and being part of a support system is a dynamic process. It's about giving and receiving, learning and growing, and, most importantly, connecting on a level that brings comfort and understanding. In our times, where change is the only constant, having a support network is not just helpful; it's essential. Through the highs and lows, the people who stand by us make the journey both bearable, enriching, and fulfilling.

Mindfulness and Meditation for Stress Management. In the whirl of everyday life, where deadlines loom and expectations soar, finding a moment of calm can feel like a distant dream. Yet, within these moments of hustle, mindfulness and meditation emerge as beacons of peace, offering tools to navigate and thrive amidst the chaos.

Basics of Mindfulness and Meditation. Mindfulness is fully present and engaged, aware of our thoughts and feelings without judgment. Meditation, often used alongside mindfulness, involves focusing on the breath or a particular idea to achieve mental clarity and emotional calm. The magic of these practices lies in their simplicity and accessibility—requiring no special equipment, they can be woven into the fabric of daily life, offering respite and rejuvenation for the mind.

The benefits of mindfulness and meditation range from reducing stress and anxiety to improving focus and emotional resilience. By anchoring us in the present, they cut through the noise of past regrets and future worries, revealing the peace in the here and now.

Simple Mindfulness Exercises. Incorporating mindfulness into your day doesn't have to be a daunting task. Here are a few exercises to get you started:

- **Mindful Breathing**: Focus solely on your breath for a few minutes daily. Notice the sensation of air entering and leaving your nostrils, your chest's rise and fall, and your breathing's rhythm.

- **Sensory Observation**: Pick an everyday activity like breakfast or walking to school. Engage fully with the experience, noticing the colors, textures, sounds, and smells. This practice enhances appreciation for the small wonders of daily life.

- **Gratitude Reflection**: At the end of each day, reflect on three things you're grateful for. This can shift your focus from what's lacking to the abundance present in your life.

Creating a Meditation Practice

Starting a meditation practice might initially seem intimidating, but it's about progress, not perfection. Here are tips for building a meditation routine that sticks:

- **Find Your Spot**: Designate a quiet, comfortable space for meditation. This can be a corner of your room, a spot on the floor with cushions, or a chair by a window. The key is consistency—the more you associate this space with meditation, the easier it becomes to enter a meditative state.

- **Set a Schedule**: Consistency is crucial. Try to meditate at the same time each day, whether first thing in the morning, during a midday break, or right before bed. Start with just a few minutes and gradually increase the time as it becomes a natural part of your routine.

- **Use Guided Meditations**: Guided meditations can be beneficial if unsure where to start. Many apps and websites offer free sessions to introduce you to meditation techniques.

Mindfulness in Daily Life. The true power of mindfulness unfolds when it extends beyond formal practice into everyday moments. Here are ways to infuse mindfulness into your daily routines:

- **Attentive Listening**: Give them your full attention when conversing with someone. Notice their expressions, tone, and the emotions behind their words. This not only enriches the interaction but also strengthens connections.

- **Mindful Eating**: Turn meals into mindful experiences. Chew slowly, savoring each bite, and pay attention to the flavors and textures. This can enhance your enjoyment of food and help you tune into your body's hunger and fullness signals.

- **Pause Between Tasks**: Before transitioning from one activity to another, pause briefly. This can be a moment of deep breathing or simply a chance to acknowledge the completion of one task before moving to the next. These pauses can serve as mini mental breaks, refreshing your mind throughout the day.

Integrating mindfulness and meditation into your life doesn't require monumental changes. It's about weaving small moments of awareness into the fabric of your day, transforming ordinary experiences into opportunities for presence, connection, and peace. These moments build upon each other through practice, creating a tapestry of mindfulness that can support and enrich your mental and emotional well-being, guiding you through life's challenges with a steadier hand and a more open heart.

Overcoming Peer Pressure: Staying True to Yourself. Navigating the social waters of adolescence often means facing the currents of peer pressure. It's like being at a crossroads where every direction seems to be marked by the expectations and influences of others. Understanding peer pressure involves recognizing its subtle and overt forms, from the urge to try something risky to the implicit feeling of needing to conform. Its impact can stretch far beyond the immediate moment, shaping decisions and affecting self-esteem.

Peer pressure thrives on the fear of exclusion, leveraging the deep-seated human need to belong. However, the desire to be part of a group should encourage you to stay in your true self. Here's how you can hold your ground:

- **Assertiveness Training**: It is crucial to learn to express your thoughts and feelings confidently. Practice saying no in a firm yet polite manner. Role-playing different scenarios with a trusted friend or adult can boost your confidence.

- **Decision-Making Skills**: Strengthen your ability to make decisions independently. Consider the consequences of your actions and whether they align with your goals and values. Pausing to reflect before acting gives you the space to choose your path, not one dictated by others.

- **Identifying Personal Values**: Knowing what you stand for is an anchor, keeping you grounded amidst external pressures. Reflect on your beliefs, principles, and what truly matters to you. This clarity can illuminate your path when peer pressure clouds your judgment.

Finding peers who respect and share your values can shield you from negative influences. Here's how to cultivate a supportive social circle:

- **Explore Interests**: Engage in clubs, teams, or online communities that reflect your passions. These spaces can connect you with individuals who share your enthusiasm and outlook.

- **Be Open**: While it's comforting to surround yourself with like-minded peers, remain open to diverse perspectives. True friends respect differences and can broaden your horizons.

- **Quality Over Quantity**: A few genuine friends offer more meaningful support than many acquaintances. Nurture these relationships through honest communication, shared experiences, and mutual respect.

In the tapestry of life, peer pressure is one thread among many. It has the potential to lead you astray, but it also offers opportunities for growth, self-discovery, and strengthening your resolve. Your responses to peer pressure can shape your journey, teaching you about integrity, courage, and the value of staying true to yourself.

As we wrap up this exploration, remember that withstanding peer pressure isn't about isolation or defiance. It's about honoring your individuality while remaining connected to others. It takes practice, patience, and, sometimes, learning from missteps. But each decision, made with intention and self-awareness, weaves a more robust, vibrant fabric of your being. With these strategies and insights, you're better equipped to navigate the complexities of adolescence, making choices that reflect your true self.

Moving forward, let's apply these lessons to the broader context of our lives, resisting peer pressure in all aspects of decision-making and relationship-building. As we step into the next chapter, we'll explore how these principles apply beyond peer influence, guiding us in creating a life that resonates with our deepest selves.

Chapter Three

Navigating Conversations with Confidence: Techniques to Speak Up and Be Heard

E ffective communication is a beacon of empowerment in the throes of high school life, where every day is a mesh of lessons learned inside and outside the classroom. It's the bridge connecting thoughts to the world, transforming silence into a symphony of expression. However, the path to wielding this power confidently can sometimes be lined with clarity. The challenge often lies not in the lack of ideas but in the hesitation that muffles voices before they're heard. This chapter delves into how you can navigate conversations with assurance, ensuring your voice isn't just part of the noise but a distinct echo that resonates.

Confidence Building. The first step to speaking up with authority is dismantling the barriers of nervousness that shackle your thoughts. Confidence isn't innate but a skill honed through understanding and practice. It begins with recognizing your right to voice your opinions and acknowledging that what you say matters. A practical strategy to bolster this belief is to start small. Engage in conversations on familiar topics where you feel more at ease. Gradually, as your comfort zone expands, so does your confidence in expressing yourself in varied scenarios. This incremental approach transforms the daunting act of speaking up into a series of manageable steps, each a victory in the quest for confidence.

Voice Modulation. Your voice is an instrument, and like any instrument, how you play it can change the impact of the melody it produces. Voice modulation — the control of volume, tone, and pace — is crucial in making your spoken words leave a mark. For instance, a steady pace can convey confidence, while varying the volume can emphasize key points, making your speech more engaging. A softer tone can draw listeners in, creating a sense of intimacy, while a louder voice can command attention. To master this, observe speakers you admire. Notice how they adjust their pitch and pace to suit their message and audience. Practice mirroring these techniques in your conversations, paying attention to the reactions you elicit. This reflection will guide you in fine-tuning your vocal delivery for maximum impact.

Practice Scenarios. Like musicians practice their scales, effective communicators practice their delivery. Crafting scenarios for practice offers a safe space to experiment with your voice and message. Start with low-stakes situations, such as discussing a favorite movie with a friend. Then, gradually move to more challenging scenarios, like presenting an idea in class or initiating a discussion at a family gathering. Each scenario should serve a specific purpose, such as asserting an opinion, asking for something you need, or sharing a personal story. The key is consistent, varied practice — the more you speak up, the more natural it becomes. Consider recording yourself to identify areas for improvement, and remember, perfection isn't the goal; progress is.

Feedback Loop. Feedback is the compass that guides your improvement in communication. It offers an external perspective on how your message is received and understood. After conversations, especially those you've practiced for, seek feedback from those you trust to be honest and constructive. Ask questions like, "Did my point come across clearly?" or "How did my tone affect the message?" This input is invaluable in identifying areas for growth and reinforcing positive habits. Additionally, self-reflection after each speaking opportunity can deepen your understanding of your communication style and how it evolves.

In cultivating the skill of confident communication, the journey is as significant as the destination. Each step taken, from building foundational confidence to refining your vocal delivery, from practicing in varied scenarios to integrating feedback, is a stride towards being heard and truly understood.

The Listening Skill: How to Truly Understand What Others Are Saying

Listening is more than just hearing words; it's about fully grasping the message. This means tuning into the words and the emotions and intentions behind them. Active listening is a skill that, when practiced, allows for deeper connections and understanding in conversations.

Active Listening. Active listening involves giving full attention to the speaker, engaging with their words, and providing feedback that shows you are genuinely committed. It's a skill that demands practice. To start, consciously focus on the speaker without planning your response while they talk. This requires patience and a willingness to put your thoughts on hold. A helpful technique is to summarize what the speaker is saying as they talk mentally. This keeps you engaged and helps you understand the message in its entirety. Additionally, asking clarifying questions or paraphrasing what was said shows the speaker you are actively involved in the conversation and care about what they share.

Non-Verbal Cues. Much of the communication is non-verbal. Attention to body language and facial expressions can offer insights into the speaker's real feelings and intentions, sometimes more than words. For instance, crossed arms might indicate defensiveness, while a lack of eye contact could suggest discomfort or evasion. Smiling, nodding, and maintaining an open posture show your engagement and encourage the speaker to be more open. Observing these non-verbal cues adds a layer of understanding that words alone might not convey.

To hone this skill, practice observing people in various settings, noting their body language and facial expressions, and guessing the emotions or messages they might be trying to convey. Compare your observations with the verbal messages and see if they align or tell a different story. This exercise sharpens your ability to read non-verbal cues accurately.

Empathetic Response. Responding with empathy shows that you understand the words and connect with the emotions behind them. It involves acknowledging the speaker's feelings, whether you agree with them or not. For example, if a friend shares a problem, you might say instead of immediately offering a solution, "That sounds tough. How are you feeling about it all?" This response validates their feelings and opens the door for deeper communication. Empathy builds trust and shows the speaker that their emotions and perspectives are valued.

Practicing empathy requires patience and a genuine interest in others' experiences. It means setting aside judgments and immersing yourself in the speaker's world. Over time, this improves your listening skills and enriches your relationships.

Listening Barriers-Several barriers can impede effective listening. Recognizing and overcoming these is crucial for meaningful communication. Common barriers include:

- **Distractions:** External noises or internal thoughts can distract you from the conversation. Minimizing distractions by choosing a quiet place for meaningful conversations or consciously redirecting your focus to the speaker can help.

- **Prejudices:** Preconceived notions about the speaker or the topic can cloud your ability to listen openly. Acknowledging and setting aside these biases allows you to fully engage with what's being said.

- **Impatience:** The urge to interrupt or finish the speaker's sentences can hinder your understanding of their message. Practicing patience and giving the speaker ample time to express themselves ensures you get the whole picture.

- **Emotional Reactivity:** Strong emotional reactions to what's being said can prevent you from listening objectively. Recognizing when you're becoming emotionally reactive and calming down before responding can improve your listening skills.

Overcoming these barriers requires mindfulness and the willingness to adjust your habits for better communication. With practice, you can transform listening from a passive to an engaging and empathetic part of your conversations.

Reading Between the Lines: Understanding Non-Verbal Cues. Regarding communication, what isn't said often holds as much weight, if not more, than the spoken words. Non-verbal cues, encompassing body language and facial expressions, serve as the unspoken dialogue that enriches the narrative of our interactions. Gaining fluency in this silent language opens a new dimension of understanding, enabling a deeper connection with those around us.

Body Language Basics. Body language, the physical manifestation of our thoughts and emotions, is a powerful tool for conveying messages without uttering a single word. Consider the difference in perception when someone speaks with their arms crossed versus when they have an open stance. The former might be interpreted as defensive or closed-off, while the latter suggests openness and receptivity. Similarly, the direction of someone's feet can indicate genuine interest; feet pointed toward you offer engagement, whereas feet directed toward the door might imply a desire to leave the conversation. These physical cues, subtle yet significant, provide invaluable insights into a person's feelings and intentions.

Facial Expressions. Our faces are canvases of emotion, capable of expressing many feelings without words. A smile can signify joy or approval, a frown can denote disapproval or sadness, and raised eyebrows may signal surprise or skepticism. The fleeting micro-expressions that dart across someone's face can reveal their true feelings, often before they've had a chance to cloak them in verbal responses. Learning to interpret these expressions accurately requires keen observation and practice but can significantly enhance one's ability to empathize and connect with others on a deeper level.

Cultural Sensitivity. While non-verbal communication is universal, its interpretation is not. Cultural norms heavily influence the meaning of certain gestures and expressions, making cultural sensitivity crucial in accurately decoding non-verbal cues. For instance, direct eye contact is considered polite and indicative of honesty in many Western cultures, yet in some Asian cultures, it might be perceived as disrespectful or confrontational. Similarly, the thumbs-up gesture, widely recognized as a sign of approval in many parts of the world, can be offensive in others. Acknowledging and respecting these cultural differences is critical to effective and empathetic communication across diverse backgrounds.

Practical Exercises. Active engagement through practical exercises can be incredibly beneficial in becoming proficient in reading non-verbal cues. Here are a few to get started:

- **People Watching:** Spend time in a public place, like a park or a café, and observe the interactions around you. Notice the body language and facial expressions of the people you see. How do their non-verbal cues complement or contradict their verbal communication?

- **Mirror Practice:** Stand before a mirror and think of different emotions – happiness, anger, surprise, fear. Try to express each emotion solely through your facial expressions. This exercise not only helps in understanding how various emotions manifest physically but also aids in recognizing them in others.

- **Role-Playing:** Engage in role-playing exercises with a friend or family member. Take turns communicating emotions or intentions non-verbally while the other guesses what's being conveyed. This can be a fun and informative way to practice interpreting non-verbal signals accurately.

- **Film Analysis:** Watch a movie or TV show with the sound off and try to infer the plot or character's emotions based solely on their non-verbal cues. This exercise sharpens observation skills and enhances the ability to read context and emotion without relying on dialogue.

Incorporating these exercises into your routine can significantly improve your ability to interpret and respond to nonverbal cues in your interactions. This skill enriches your relationships and enhances effectiveness in any communicative context, from casual conversations to formal presentations and negotiations.

Conflict Resolution 101: Turning Arguments into Constructive Discussions

Conflict is a natural part of human relationships, stemming from differences in opinions, desires, and needs. While viewing conflict negatively is easy, it can catalyze growth and understanding when appropriately navigated. The key lies in transforming disputes into open dialogue and mutual understanding opportunities.

Understanding Conflict. At its core, conflict arises from differences that need to be adequately addressed or respected. It could sprout from something as simple as a misunderstanding or as complex as clashing values. Recognizing that conflict is not inherently harmful but a sign of diverse perspectives can shift how we approach resolution. It's an invitation to explore these differences and find common ground rather than a battleground for proving who's right or wrong.

Communication Strategies. Effective communication is the bridge that transforms conflict into constructive conversation. Here are strategies that can help:

- **Active Listening** means understanding the other person's viewpoint without immediately formulating a rebuttal. This requires patience and openness, qualities that signal respect and a willingness to find solutions.

- **Use "I" Statements:** Express your feelings and thoughts using "I" statements rather than "you" statements, which can come across as accusatory. For instance, "I feel upset when my ideas are dismissed" instead of "You always dismiss my ideas."

- **Clarify Misunderstandings:** Often, conflicts escalate due to misunderstandings. Asking for clarifications before responding can prevent unnecessary escalation.

- **Control Emotional Responses:** Emotions can easily take the wheel during conflicts. Taking deep breaths and pausing before responding can help maintain a level head and keep the conversation productive.

Problem-Solving Together. Finding solutions that benefit everyone involved is the goal of effective conflict resolution. This collaborative approach encourages all parties to contribute to the solution, fostering a sense of ownership and satisfaction with the outcome. Here are steps to facilitate this process:

- **Define the Problem Clearly:** Ensure everyone has the same understanding of the issue. This avoids solving the wrong problem or addressing only symptoms rather than the root cause.

- **Brainstorm Solutions Together:** Encourage all parties to propose solutions. This brainstorming phase should be judgment-free, and every suggestion should be considered.

- **Evaluate Options:** Once all suggestions are on the table, evaluate their feasibility, potential impact, and how well they address the needs of all involved.

- **Agree on a Solution:** Select the option that best meets the parties' interests. This may require compromise from everyone, but the focus should remain on the most equitable outcome.

Maintaining Respect. Maintaining respect for each other, even in disagreement, is crucial for healthy conflict resolution. It ensures that even when opinions diverge, the value of the relationship remains intact. Here are ways to keep discussions respectful:

- **Avoid Blame:** Assigning blame can escalate conflict and hurt feelings. Focus on the issue, not the person.

- **Keep an Open Mind:** Being open to the idea that you might not have all the answers or that your perspective might change fosters a respectful environment for dialogue.

- **Respect Boundaries:** Recognize when a break from the discussion is needed, either because emotions are running high or additional time is required to think things through.

- **Agree to Disagree:** Sometimes, agreeing to disagree is the most respectful outcome. It acknowledges that while a consensus may not be reachable, the perspectives of all involved are valid.

Navigating conflict to reach a constructive resolution can strengthen relationships and lead to better mutual understanding. By applying these strategies, conversations around disagreements can become opportunities for growth rather than sources of division.

Digital Communication: The Do's and Don'ts of Texting and Social Media. As a significant chunk of our interactions migrate to the digital realm, understanding the nuances of digital communication has become indispensable. Although texts and social media posts may seem straightforward, they carry layers of meaning and potential implications. Navigating this landscape tactfully can enhance your relationships, safeguard your reputation, and protect you from the darker aspects of online interaction.

Crafting Messages. When crafting messages, clarity and respect form the bedrock of effective communication. In a text devoid of facial expressions or tone of voice, your words carry the entire weight of your message. Here's how to ensure they convey precisely what you intend:

- **Be Concise**: Get straight to the point. Long-winded messages can lose their essence and confuse the reader.

- **Use Emojis Wisely**: Emojis can add color and clarify intent, but overuse or inappropriate use can dilute your message or, worse, miscommunicate your feelings.

- **Proofread:** Autocorrect mishaps or typos can sometimes wholly change a message's meaning. A quick review before sending can save you from potential embarrassment or misunderstandings.

- **Tone Awareness:** Texts can easily be misinterpreted without the cues of face-to-face conversation. If a message is essential, consider how it might be received. Could it seem harsher than intended? If there's any doubt, rephrase.

Social Media Etiquette. Social media platforms offer unparalleled connectivity and demand new behavioral norms. Here's how to navigate these spaces with grace:

- **Think Before You Post:** Every post contributes to the digital persona others perceive. Ask yourself, "Is this something I'd be comfortable with everyone seeing?"

- **Respect Privacy:** Not everyone appreciates having their moments shared online. Always ask for consent before posting pictures or details involving others.

- **Avoid Public Disputes:** Disagreements happen but airing them in a public forum rarely resolves the issue and often escalates the conflict. If you have a problem with someone, it's better to reach out privately.

- **Mind Your Tags:** Tagging friends in humorous or embarrassing content might seem innocent but can make them uncomfortable. When in doubt, ask before tagging.

Digital Footprint Awareness. Every digital interaction leaves a trace, contributing to a composite picture of who you are online – your digital footprint. This footprint can have far-reaching implications:

- **Future Implications:** Colleges, potential employers, and romantic interests might peruse your digital footprint. Posts that seem harmless now can take on a different light years later.

- **Permanence:** The internet rarely forgets. Deleted posts can often be retrieved or might have been screenshots before removal. Assume anything you post could be permanent.

- **Privacy Settings:** Regularly review the privacy settings on your social media accounts. Platforms often update their policies and settings, which could affect who can see your posts or personal information.

Cyberbullying Awareness. Cyberbullying represents one of the most concerning aspects of digital communication. Recognizing and addressing it is critical to maintaining healthy online spaces:

- **Recognize the Signs:** Cyberbullying can take many forms, from direct messages to public posts or exclusion from digital groups. The impact on mental health can be profound, so recognizing when it's happening is the first step to stopping it.

- **Respond Appropriately:** If you're the target of cyberbullying, remember that responding in kind rarely resolves the situation and can escalate it. Instead, document the bullying, block the bully, and report the behavior to the platform. If the bullying is severe or persistent, involve a trusted adult.

- **Support Others:** If you see someone else being bullied, offer your support. Sometimes, knowing they're not alone can make all the difference to someone facing harassment.

- **Promote Positivity:** Be a force for good online. Encourage positive interactions, support others, and report negative behavior. A healthier digital environment starts with each user's actions.

Navigating digital communication effectively requires clarity, respect, and awareness. By crafting clear and respectful messages, adhering to social media etiquette, being mindful of your digital footprint, and standing against cyberbullying, you can foster positive interactions and protect yourself and others from the pitfalls of online communication.

Chapter Four

Using Technology to Your Advantage

Picture this: you're holding a smartphone, swiping through a sea of apps, each with its promise of making life easier, more enjoyable, or even more fun. It's like having a Swiss Army knife in your digital pocket, but instead of a blade or a screwdriver, you've got tools to learn new languages, solve complex equations, or dive into the universe's wonders. This chapter is about turning your digital devices into powerful allies in your quest for knowledge, focusing on educational apps that teach, engage, and entertain.

Educational Apps That Make Learning Fun App Selection. Choosing the right educational app can feel like finding a needle in a haystack. With thousands available, how do you pick the ones that benefit you? Start with clarity about what you want to achieve. Are you looking to improve your math skills, learn a new language, or grasp historical events? Once pinpointing your learning goals, look for apps with high ratings and positive user reviews.

These are often good indicators of quality and effectiveness. Also, check if the app offers a trial period or a free version to test it out before fully committing.

Diverse Learning Tools. There's an app for almost every subject under the sun. For languages, apps like Duolingo use gamification to make learning new words and grammar less daunting and more fun. If math is your focus, Photomath allows you to scan math problems for instant explanations of how to solve them. For those intrigued by science, apps like Star Walk 2 provide an interactive guide to the night sky, turning astronomy into an engaging, hands-on experience. For coders in the making, platforms like Codecademy and Scratch offer user-friendly ways to get started with programming, making what seems complex more accessible and enjoyable.

Gamified Learning. The beauty of gamified learning apps lies in their ability to turn education into an adventure. Earning points, unlocking levels, and receiving virtual rewards make learning feel more like a game and less like a chore. This approach makes studying more engaging and enhances motivation and retention. Studies have shown that gamification can lead to higher levels of engagement and achievement in learners. When choosing an app, look for those that balance fun and educational content, ensuring that while you're playing, you're also learning.

Staying Updated. Educational apps are constantly evolving, with new tools and updates released regularly. Updating the latest apps can help you use the most advanced learning technologies. Follow tech blogs, join online forums focused on educational technology, or subscribe to newsletters covering the latest app developments. This way, you'll be among the first to know about new apps that can enhance your learning experience or updates that add exciting features to the ones you already use.

Organizing Your Life: Tech Tools for Time Management. In a world where every second counts, staying on top of your schedule can feel like trying to catch raindrops in your hands—possible but tricky without the right tools. This is where digital planners and calendars come into play, turning the daunting task of juggling multiple commitments into a manageable, even enjoyable, process. Let's explore the digital solutions that can transform how you organize your life, ensuring you never miss a beat.

Digital Planners and Calendars. Gone are the days of scribbling notes on paper calendars or trying to remember appointments off the top of your head. Digital planners and calendars offer a sleek, efficient way to keep track of your daily, weekly, and monthly obligations. Apps like Google Calendar and Microsoft Outlook provide platforms where you can color-code different types of events for quick reference, set recurring appointments for routine commitments, and even share your schedule with others to simplify planning group activities or family outings. For a more visually appealing approach, apps such as Fantastical or TimeTree present your schedule in innovative formats, incorporating weather forecasts or allowing for collaborative planning with friends, classmates, or coworkers.

Task Management Apps. While digital calendars keep you aware of the 'when,' task management apps tackle the 'what.' These apps are designed to break your workload into bite-sized pieces, making even the most overwhelming projects less daunting. Trello uses a card-based system that allows you to categorize tasks, set deadlines, and track progress visually. Similarly, Asana organizes tasks into projects, with options to add due dates, assignees, and custom labels, ensuring every detail of your project is accounted for. For those who prefer a minimalist approach, Todoist offers a straightforward, list-based interface with powerful features hiding beneath its simple exterior, such as natural language processing for quick task entry and productivity tracking to monitor your progress over time.

Setting Reminders. Remembering to check your planner or task list is a task in itself. This is where reminder apps shine, nudging you about upcoming deadlines or scheduled activities so nothing slips through the cracks. Apps like Due specialize in persistent reminders that keep notifying you at intervals you set until you mark the task as done. While primarily a note-taking app, Google Keep allows you to attach reminders to your notes, making it perfect for those quick thoughts or tasks you need to remember at specific times or places. Integrating these reminder apps into your daily routine ensures you stay one step ahead of your responsibilities, freeing up mental space for more critical or creative endeavors.

The Importance of Digital Detox. As much as technology can aid in managing our time more effectively, it's crucial to recognize the value of unplugging regularly. The constant barrage of notifications and the temptation to check just one more email before bed can lead to digital burnout, diminishing the productivity these tools seek to enhance. Setting aside times to disconnect from digital devices—during meals, an hour before sleep, or designated tech-free weekends—can help restore balance. This practice prevents overwhelming and encourages you to engage more deeply with the world around you, fostering creativity, relaxation, and a greater appreciation for the moments that technology can't capture.

In navigating the landscape of digital tools designed to streamline our lives, it's clear that with the right approach, technology can be a powerful ally in mastering the art of time management. From elegantly organized calendars that keep our schedules in check, task management apps that break down our goals into achievable steps, and reminder systems that ensure we're always on top of our game, these tools collectively offer a roadmap to a more organized, productive, and balanced life.

Building a Positive Online Presence: Tips for Teens. The World Wide Web is a vast and varied landscape, filled with opportunities to express yourself, share your achievements, and connect with others who share your interests. Creating an online space that accurately reflects who they are and what they stand for is more critical than ever for teens today. Here, we explore how to craft an online identity that aligns with their real-world self, showcasing their unique talents and accomplishments while navigating the digital realm safely and smartly.

Defining Your Digital Identity. Think of your digital identity as your brand. What message do you want to tell the world about who you are? Whether you're passionate about environmental activism, a wizard with coding, or an aspiring artist, your online presence should mirror these interests and values. Start by considering the adjectives you would like people to associate with you when they come across your profile. Creative? Driven? Compassionate? Use these traits as a guide to curate content that reflects this image. For instance, if creativity is a trait you cherish, share your artwork, write about your creative process, or post about the artists who inspire you.

Showcasing Talents and Achievements. Social media and personal websites are potent tools for highlighting your skills and successes. Did you recently win a science fair? Volunteer at a local charity event? Or finish a project you're particularly proud of? Share these milestones! They glimpse your passion and demonstrate your commitment and achievements to friends, family, and potential future employers or colleagues. Consider creating a digital portfolio on platforms like Behance for artwork or GitHub for coding projects, which allows you to compile and showcase your work professionally and organizationally.

- **Create a consistent theme: Whether through a specific color scheme, type of content, or tone of voice, maintaining consistency helps reinforce your digital identity.**

- **Use hashtags wisely: They can increase the visibility of your posts to like-minded communities but avoid overusing them or incorporating irrelevant ones.**

- **Engage with your audience: Respond to comments and messages to build a rapport with your followers. Interaction adds a personal touch and fosters a sense of community around your online presence.**

Networking Online. Expanding your digital horizons can lead to meaningful connections and opportunities. Start by following and interacting with professionals and influencers in your areas of interest. Comment on their posts, share their content (with credit), and don't hesitate to reach out with thoughtful questions or contributions to discussions. Joining groups and forums related to your interests can also be a great way to meet others who share your passions and can offer advice, support, and collaboration opportunities. LinkedIn, for example, is not just for job seekers; it's a platform where you can connect with professionals and join groups to stay updated on industry news, trends, and opportunities.

- **Personalize connection requests:** Always include a personalized message when contacting professionals or new contacts. It significantly improves response rates compared to generic requests.

- **Be an active participant:** Contribute meaningfully to conversations in groups or forums. Share your insights, ask questions, and provide feedback. Active participation can establish you as a thoughtful and engaged community member.

Safety and Privacy. While building your online presence, keeping your personal information secure and managing your privacy settings should always be a priority. Oversharing personal details can put your privacy at risk and affect how others perceive your digital identity.

- **Review privacy settings regularly:** Social media platforms often update their privacy policies and settings. Make it a habit to review and adjust your settings to ensure you're comfortable with what you share and with whom.

- **Think before you share:** Consider whether sharing sensitive personal information like your address, phone number, or details about your daily routine could compromise your privacy or safety before posting anything.

- **Use solid and unique passwords:** Protect your accounts with passwords that are difficult to guess. Consider using a password manager to keep track of them.

- **Be cautious with friend requests:** Accept requests only from people you know. If you're unsure about a request, ignoring or declining it is safer than risking your privacy.

Building a positive online presence is more than curating a feed or accumulating followers. It's an ongoing process of expressing your identity, connecting with others, and navigating the digital world with intention and integrity. By thoughtfully crafting your digital identity, showcasing your achievements, networking with purpose, and prioritizing your safety and privacy, you lay the groundwork for an online presence that reflects who you are and propels you toward the future you envision.

The Creative Side of Technology: Exploring Digital Arts and Coding

Digital creativity offers a playground for the imagination, where art meets the infinite possibilities of technology. This section ventures into how technology can amplify artistic expression and innovation, guiding you through tools and platforms that bring digital art to life, the significance of coding skills in creative endeavors, and ways to share and collaborate on digital projects.

Digital Art Platforms. Digital art transforms traditional canvases into dynamic screens, where brushes become styluses and colors are as limitless as pixels can render. Various platforms cater to artists at every skill level, from novices looking to dabble in digital drawings to professionals creating complex 3D models. Adobe Creative Cloud remains a powerhouse with tools like Photoshop for image editing and Illustrator for vector art. For those starting, Procreate offers a user-friendly interface with robust features for drawing and painting on iPads. Meanwhile, Blender opens the door to 3D modeling and animation, offering free access to tools that can bring sculptures and characters to life in a digital space. Each platform has its community and resources, providing tutorials and forums where artists can learn, share, and grow.

Learning to Code. In today's digital world, understanding the language of computers—coding—has become a valuable skill across various fields, including the arts. Coding offers a toolset for creating interactive art, developing video games, or designing complex websites showcasing your digital portfolio. For those curious about coding, several resources make this skill accessible and engaging. Codecademy and Khan Academy offer free courses on languages suited for the web, like HTML, CSS, and JavaScript, which are ideal for beginners. Scratch, a platform developed by MIT, introduces younger learners to coding through a visual interface where users can create animations and games through simple block-based programming. These skills open up new dimensions for creative expression, where your artwork can interact with viewers in novel and immersive ways.

Creative Projects. Combining art and technology can lead to innovative projects that push the boundaries of both fields. Digital storytelling, for instance, uses multimedia elements—text, images, sound, and video—to tell stories in engaging ways that traditional books or oral storytelling cannot match. Apps like Adobe Spark make creating and sharing these stories easy, offering templates and tools for crafting narratives enriched with visual and auditory elements. Video game design is another area where art and coding intersect. Platforms like Unity or Unreal Engine provide the groundwork for developing games, from simple 2D puzzles to complex 3D environments, allowing artists and coders to bring their visions to interactive life. These projects provide a creative outlet for learning and applying digital skills in real-world scenarios.

Sharing Creativity. The digital age has made sharing and collaborating on creative projects more accessible. Platforms like DeviantArt and Behance allow artists to showcase their work to a global audience, receive feedback, and connect with fellow creatives. When sharing your work online, consider the following tips to ensure a positive and productive experience:

- **Protect Your Work:** Use watermarks or share images at a lower resolution to prevent unauthorized use.

- **Engage with Your Community:** Respond to comments, participate in challenges, and support other artists. Building relationships can lead to collaborations and opportunities.

- **Be Open to Feedback:** Constructive criticism can be invaluable for growth. Listen to what others say about your work and trust your artistic vision.

For collaborations, tools like Google Drive or Dropbox simplify sharing files and working on projects together, regardless of distance. Trello or Slack can help manage projects, allowing teams to communicate effectively and keep track of progress. These collaborations can lead to unique projects that might not have been possible individually, highlighting the power of collective creativity in the digital age. By embracing technology's creative side, artists and coders unlock new realms of possibility. From crafting digital art and learning the fundamentals of coding to embarking on innovative projects and sharing them with the world, technology enhances creative expression. It connects us to a vast digital canvas of shared imagination and innovation.

Virtual Volunteering: Making a Difference from Your Device. In a world where digital connections often transcend geographical boundaries, the concept of volunteering has evolved. Virtual volunteering, which is no longer confined to local soup kitchens or community centers, allows giving back from the comfort of one's home. This shift opens many opportunities for those eager to contribute and allows for a personalized approach to philanthropy, matching skills, and interests with global needs.

Finding Virtual Volunteering Opportunities. The first step in your virtual volunteering voyage is discovering opportunities that align with your passions and skills. Numerous platforms like VolunteerMatch and Idealist.org offer filters to narrow search results to remote opportunities. Additionally, United Nations Volunteers and Catchafire focus on matching professionals with nonprofits needing specific skill sets, from graphic design to legal consulting. When searching, consider the causes you're passionate about—education, environmental conservation, or health—and use these as guiding stars to find your perfect match.

Making an Impact Remotely. The scope of virtual volunteering is as vast as the internet itself, covering various activities that can make a real-world difference. Online tutoring through platforms like Khan Academy allows volunteers to support students from anywhere in the world in subjects they excel in. Digital advocacy campaigns leverage social media to raise awareness about critical issues, engaging a broader audience than traditional methods. For instance, translators Without Borders relies on volunteers to translate medical texts or crisis response information, breaking down language barriers in global emergencies. These examples illustrate how virtual volunteering can extend your impact beyond your local community.

Building Skills Through Volunteering. Aside from the generous benefits, virtual volunteering offers a unique personal and professional growth avenue. Engaging in projects that require you to utilize or expand your skill set can add valuable experience to your resume or college application. For instance, managing a nonprofit's social media campaign can enhance your digital marketing skills, while developing a mobile app for a charity can showcase your coding prowess. This symbiotic relationship not only furthers your career goals but also amplifies the impact of your volunteer work, creating a win-win scenario.

Connecting with Global Communities. One of the most profound benefits of virtual volunteering is connecting with people from various cultures and walks of life. This interaction fosters a sense of global citizenship, an understanding that our actions can have a ripple effect worldwide. Contributing to projects in different countries broadens your perspective, encouraging empathy, cultural sensitivity, and a deeper appreciation for the challenges others face. It's a reminder that compassion knows no borders in our increasingly interconnected world.

In wrapping up this exploration of virtual volunteering, it's clear that the digital age has transformed giving back, making it more accessible, flexible, and aligned with our skills and interests. The opportunities to make a difference from your device are endless, from tutoring students online to contributing to global advocacy campaigns. This approach extends our impact beyond our immediate surroundings and offers a pathway for personal growth and global connection. As we look ahead, the potential for virtual volunteering to shape a more compassionate, connected world is immense, underscoring the power of digital platforms to bring about positive change.

If you or someone you know are raising children in this fast-paced crazy world, then you know how important it is to get them started in the right direction. If just a few chapters of this book would help them in their day-to-day lives, then I would be highly honored if you would first scroll up and ''Buy Now With 1-Click'' This book might make a massive difference in the lives of many young people if they can find it. Please take a few minutes and leave an honest review on The Amazon Page. You might think that one review wouldn't matter, but it does. The more reviews this book has, the greater the chance it will be ranked higher on the Amazon page, making it more likely to be found by anyone needing it.

I cannot thank you enough, and I am eternally grateful that you are reading this book. I hope it helps your teenager with their day-to-day struggles. Scroll up, Click <u>"Buy Now With 1-Click"</u> and

<u>Get them reading now!</u>

Chapter Five

Building Emotional Intelligence

Self-Reflection Practices. Self-reflection is like standing back to watch the waves, contemplating their beauty and power from a distance. It allows you to observe your emotional responses without getting swept away. Here are some practices to enhance self-reflection:

- **Ask Yourself Why:** When an emotion arises, ask yourself, "Why do I feel this way?" Digging into the root cause of your feelings can offer profound insights.

- **Consider the Impact:** Reflect on how your emotions influence your thoughts, decisions, and interactions with others. Are they serving you well, or do they often lead you astray?

- **Seek Feedback:** Sometimes, an outside perspective can

shed light on aspects of our emotional landscape we might overlook. Trusted friends or family members can offer valuable insights into how your emotions manifest and affect those around you.

Mindfulness Techniques. Mindfulness is about being fully present in the moment, riding the wave of your emotions without judgment. Here are some mindfulness techniques that can help you become more attuned to your emotional state:

- **Focused Breathing:** When emotions surge, take a moment to focus on your breath. Deep, slow breaths can help calm the mind, making it easier to observe your feelings without getting overwhelmed.

- **Mindful Observation:** Spend a few minutes each day observing your surroundings or internal state without judgment. This practice can improve your ability to remain present and aware, even in emotionally charged situations.

- **Body Scan Meditation:** This involves mentally scanning your body for areas of tension or discomfort, which can indicate emotional stress. Acknowledging these areas and consciously relaxing them can also help release emotional tension.

By recognizing and understanding your emotions, journaling to track your feelings, engaging in self-reflection, and practicing mindfulness, you're setting the foundation for a healthy emotional life. These strategies enhance your emotional intelligence and empower you to navigate the complex seas of human emotion with confidence and poise.

Managing Stress Before It Manages You: Practical Stress Reduction Techniques Stress can seem inevitable in a world filled with deadlines, expectations, and constant digital notifications. However, recognizing its effects and implementing strategies to mitigate its grip can transform stress from a daunting shadow into a manageable aspect of everyday life.

Understanding Stress. Stress, in its essence, activates our body's 'fight or flight' response, preparing us for perceived threats. This reaction can be beneficial, providing the necessary energy to tackle challenges. However, when stress becomes chronic, it can lead to both physiological issues, like headaches and high blood pressure, and psychological ones, such as anxiety and depression. The key lies in identifying when stress stops being a helpful motivator and starts being a hindrance to our well-being.

Relaxation Techniques

Relaxation techniques serve as anchors to counter the tide of stress, grounding us and providing a sense of calm amidst the chaos. Here are a few methods to consider:

- **Deep Breathing Exercises:** Simple yet effective, deep breathing can help lower stress levels immediately. Focusing on slow, deep breaths can reduce heart rate and blood pressure, signaling to your body that it's time to relax.

- **Meditation:** Meditation encourages focused attention and awareness, helping to clear the clutter of daily worries and stress. Even a few minutes a day can significantly affect overall stress levels.

- **Progressive Muscle Relaxation:** This technique involves tensing each muscle group in the body tightly, but not to the point of strain, and slowly relaxing them. This process can help identify areas of tension and encourage relaxation throughout the body.

Time Management Skills

One of the most common sources of stress is feeling overwhelmed by too many commitments or tasks. Developing practical time management skills can help to alleviate this pressure:

- **Prioritizing Tasks:** Not all tasks are created equal. Identifying what needs immediate attention and what can wait is crucial. This not only helps reduce stress but also achieves more in less time.

- **Breaking Tasks into Smaller Steps:** Large projects can seem overwhelming. Breaking them into manageable steps makes them less daunting and more accessible.

- **Setting Boundaries:** It's essential to know when to say no. Overcommitting can lead to burnout, and setting clear boundaries about what you can and cannot do is vital in managing stress.

Healthy Lifestyle Choices

The foundation of stress management lies in maintaining a healthy lifestyle. The choices we make every day can either act as stressors or as tools for stress reduction:

- **Regular Exercise:** Physical activity releases endorphins, chemicals in the brain that act as natural painkillers and mood elevators. Incorporating regular exercise into your routine can significantly reduce stress.

- **Quality Sleep:** Sleep and stress have a two-way relationship. Stress can lead to sleepless nights, and lack of sleep can increase stress levels. Establishing a healthy sleep routine can help break this cycle.

- **Balanced Diet:** What we eat affects how we feel. A diet rich in fruits, vegetables, lean proteins, and whole grains can provide the energy to tackle stressors effectively.

Incorporating these strategies into your daily life can help manage stress and enhance your overall well-being. Remember, stress is a part of life, but it doesn't have to control it. By taking proactive steps, you can reduce its impact and navigate life's challenges with a clearer mind and a healthier body.

The Power of Empathy: Understanding and Connecting with Others

Empathy stands at the crossroads of emotional intelligence, a vital tool for navigating the intricate web of human relationships. It moves beyond mere understanding to a shared experience, feeling what another person feels as if their emotions were yours. This profound connection fosters trust and intimacy, laying the groundwork for genuine relationships.

Defining Empathy. At its core, empathy is the ability to perceive and relate to the feelings and perspectives of others. It goes beyond sympathy —feeling for someone — to feeling with them, stepping into their shoes, and experiencing their emotions. This ability is crucial for building meaningful connections because it breaks down isolation barriers, creating a bridge of under-standing and compassion between individuals.

Developing Empathy. Empathy might come more natu-rally to some than others, but it is a skill that can be culti-vated with intention and practice. Here are some strategies to strengthen your empathetic abilities:

- **Active Listening:** Focus intently on what the other person is saying without formulating a response or judgment. This attentiveness signals that you value their perspective and genuinely try to understand their experience.

- **Perspective-Taking:** Make a conscious effort to see situations from the other person's viewpoint. This can be as simple as asking yourself, "How would I feel in their situation?" or "What might be influencing their feelings about this?"

- **Curiosity About Others:** Cultivate a genuine inter-est in others' experiences and feelings. Ask open-ended questions, encouraging them to share their thoughts and emotions.

- **Empathy Mapping:** Create an "empathy map" for someone you want to understand better. Divide a pa-per into sections for what they think, feel, see, and do. Fill these sections with your observations and insights, focusing on capturing their experience as fully as pos-sible.

Empathy in Action. Incorporating empathy into daily inter-actions can significantly impact your relationships. Here are some practical ways to demonstrate empathy:

- **Validate Feelings:** Let the other person know their feelings are understandable and valid, even if you might have reacted differently in the same situation. A simple "It makes sense you'd feel that way" can be profoundly affirming.

- **Offer Support:** Sometimes, empathizing means offering support through help, encouragement, or being there. It's about showing the other person they're not alone in what they're going through.

- **Reflect Emotions:** Gently reflect the emotions you sense from the other person. This could be through verbal affirmations or non-verbal cues like nodding. It signals that you're engaged and empathetic to their situation.

- **Share Vulnerably:** When appropriate, sharing your own similar experiences — without overshadowing their moment — can deepen the empathetic connection. It's saying, "I've been there too, and I understand."

The Limits of Empathy. While empathy is a powerful tool for connection, it's also essential to recognize its limits and the importance of boundary-setting to prevent empathy fatigue. This occurs when the emotional cost of constantly empathizing with others leads to burnout, leaving you emotionally depleted. Here are some tips for maintaining healthy boundaries:

- **Self-Care:** Regularly engage in self-care practices that replenish your emotional reserves. Remember, you can't pour it from an empty cup.

- **Learn to Detach:** Practice detaching yourself from the emotional weight of others' experiences. This doesn't mean you care any less, but it allows you to offer empathy without becoming overwhelmed.

- **Recognize Your Limits:** Understand that it's okay not always to have the emotional bandwidth to extend empathy. It's better to set a boundary than to offer support half-heartedly.

- **Seek Support:** As you offer empathy to others, allow yourself to receive it. Sharing the emotional load with trusted friends or family can help you recharge.

Empathy can transform how you relate to others and navigate the world when balanced with self-preservation. It's about understanding and connecting on a deeply human level, recognizing the shared emotions that bind us all. Through developing and practicing empathy, you can build stronger, more meaningful relationships and foster a sense of community and understanding that enriches your life and those around you.

Building Resilience: Overcoming Setbacks with Grace. Life throws curveballs and unexpected challenges that can either break or build us. At the heart of navigating these twists and turns with poise is resilience. This quality isn't about avoiding difficulties; instead, it's about facing them head-on, learning, and emerging more substantial on the other side. Resilience is the inner strength that fuels recovery and fosters growth in the face of adversity.

Understanding Resilience. Resilience is often viewed as the ability to bounce back from setbacks, but it's much more. It involves adapting well in the face of trauma, tragedy, threats, or significant sources of stress. It's the process of harnessing resources to sustain well-being. This quality doesn't eliminate stress or erase life's difficulties but allows individuals to tackle them more effectively and maintain their equilibrium. Recognizing that resilience is not a trait people have or do not have is crucial. It involves behaviors, thoughts, and actions that anyone can develop.

Resilience-Building Strategies. Building resilience is akin to muscle strengthening; it requires time, effort, and the right exercises. Here are strategies that can fortify your resilience:

- **Set Realistic Goals:** Break your larger goals into smaller, manageable tasks. Achieving these smaller tasks can provide a sense of accomplishment and a confidence boost, making it easier to tackle more significant challenges.

- **Maintain a Positive Outlook:** Keeping an optimistic outlook doesn't mean ignoring reality. It's about maintaining a hopeful perspective and focusing on what you can control. Practice visualizing what you want rather than worrying about what you fear.

- **Develop Problem-Solving Skills:** When faced with a setback, take a step back to assess the situation. Identify possible solutions and create a plan of action. This proactive approach can reduce feelings of powerlessness and build your problem-solving toolkit.

- **Embrace Change:** Flexibility is a critical component of resilience. Adaptability in the face of change makes it easier to adjust to new realities and find the silver lining in challenging situations.

Learning from Failure. Mistakes and failures are inevitable, but they're also invaluable learning opportunities. Here's how embracing failure can enhance your resilience:

- **Reframe Failure:** View failures as lessons, not losses. Each mistake is a chance to learn and grow. Ask yourself, "What can I learn from this experience?"

- **Celebrate Effort:** Recognize your effort to pursue your goals, regardless of the outcome. Effort is something within your control, and acknowledging it fosters resilience.

- **Seek Feedback:** Constructive feedback can provide insights into areas for improvement. It's about understanding how you can do better next time.

Support Systems. A robust support system plays a pivotal role in building and sustaining resilience. Friends, family, mentors, and community resources can offer encouragement, advice, and practical assistance in tough times. Here's how you can cultivate and lean on your support network:

- **Reach Out:** Don't hesitate to ask for help when needed. Letting others in can provide different perspectives and solutions you might have yet to consider.

- **Offer Support:** Be there for others in their time of need. Offering support can strengthen your relationships and build a community of mutual aid.

- **Engage in Group Activities:** Participating in group activities, whether a sports team, a hobby club, or a volunteer group, can provide a sense of belonging and an additional layer of support.

Building resilience is a dynamic process that requires patience and persistence. You can face life's challenges with resilience and grace by setting realistic goals, maintaining a positive outlook, developing problem-solving skills, embracing change, learning from failure, and nurturing a solid support system.

From Frustration to Patience: A Teen's Guide to Emotional Regulation.

Navigating the waters of teenage years often means dealing with a sea of emotions, where frustration and anger can sometimes seem like the dominating waves. Yet, understanding how to transform these intense feelings into patience and calmness not only smooths out the rough seas but also sets the sail for healthier relationships and personal growth. Let's explore how you can steer through these emotional tides.

Recognizing Triggers. The first step in navigating through frustration is pinpointing what sets off these strong emotions. Triggers are unique to everyone, ranging from specific situations and words to actions of others or even internal thoughts. Gaining clarity on these triggers involves a bit of detective work. Pay close attention to the moments when frustration begins to bubble up. What happened right before? Was it something someone said, a particular event, or even a thought that crossed your mind? Keeping a note of these instances can help you identify patterns and, more importantly, allow you to prepare for or even avoid certain trigger situations in the future.

Developing Patience. Transforming frustration into patience isn't about suppressing your feelings but learning to manage them to benefit you and those around you. Here are a few techniques to foster patience:

- **Pause and Breathe:** When you feel frustration rising, give yourself a moment to pause. Take a few deep breaths to help calm your mind and body, giving you space to respond rather than react.

- **Reframe the Situation:** Try to view frustrating situations from a different angle. Asking yourself questions like, "Is there another way to look at this?" or "Will this matter in the long run?" can help put things into perspective.

- **Practice Gratitude:** Shifting your focus to the positive aspects of your life or the current situation can help mitigate feelings of frustration. Regularly reflecting on things you're grateful for can cultivate a more patient and positive outlook.

Emotional Coping Strategies

Healthy coping strategies are crucial to constructively managing frustration and anger. Here are some effective methods:

- **Express Yourself:** Talking about your feelings with someone you trust can provide relief and often offers new insights or solutions. Writing down your thoughts can be therapeutic if talking isn't an option.

- **Engage in Physical Activity:** Exercise is a powerful outlet for frustration. Physical activity can reduce stress, improve mood, and give you a break from whatever is causing your frustration.

- **Seek Creative Outlets:** Creative activities like drawing, music, or writing can offer a way to express and process your emotions, turning feelings of frustration into works of art or creative projects.

Long-Term Benefits

Mastering emotional regulation, notably transforming frustration into patience, has significant long-term benefits that ripple through all aspects of life. It lays the groundwork for healthier and more fulfilling personal and professional relationships, as people are naturally drawn to people who can comfortably handle challenging situations. Moreover, developing patience strengthens your problem-solving skills, as it allows you the space to think clearly and make more thoughtful decisions. Lastly, it contributes to your overall well-being, as managing frustration effectively can reduce stress and its associated health risks.

As we wrap up this exploration of emotional regulation, remember that learning to navigate through feelings of frustration and anger is a journey. It's about equipping yourself with the tools to respond to life's challenges with patience and understanding.

These skills enhance your personal growth and relationships and prepare you for the complex emotional landscapes you may encounter. With practice and perseverance, you can transform how you experience and react to frustration, opening the door to a more patient and resilient version of yourself.

As we move forward, remember the significance of emotional regulation in building a foundation for robust emotional intelligence. The strategies and insights are stepping stones to a more emotionally aware and resilient self.

Chapter Six

Digital Literacy and Safety

I magine your online world as a bustling city: streets lined with information, intersections with social gatherings, and signs flashing with the latest news and trends. Like any city, navigating it safely requires knowing the rules of the road, the safe paths to travel, and how to protect your valuables from pickpockets. In this digital city, your personal information is the treasure you're carrying. Let's equip you with the skills to move around this city safely, keeping your treasure secure from those lurking in the shadows.

Cyber Smarts: Keeping Your Information Safe Online Understanding Cyber Risks. The risk of stumbling into a digital pothole is real. Phishing scams, where tricksters fish for your personal information through seemingly legitimate requests, and malware, software designed to harm your device or steal your data, are our digital city's potholes and open maintenance holes. Recognizing these dangers is the first step to avoiding them. For instance, an email from your 'bank' asking for your account details or a download link from an unknown source should raise immediate red flags.

Creating Strong Passwords. Think of passwords as the keys to your digital home. You wouldn't want someone quickly copying them. Strong, unique passwords are your first defense against intruders. Here are some tips for creating robust passwords:

- **Mix it up:** Use a combination of letters (both upper and lower case), numbers, and symbols.

- **Length matters:** Aim for at least 12 characters. The longer, the more potent.

- **Avoid the obvious:** Birthdays, pet names, or sequential numbers are easily guessable.

- **Use a passphrase:** Consider a random collection of words you can remember but others wouldn't guess.

- **Manager tools:** Password managers can generate and store complex passwords for you, so you don't have to memorize them.

Privacy Settings. Your social media accounts are like houses on this busy street. Adjusting your privacy settings helps you control who can knock on your door and who can peek through the windows. Most platforms offer a range of settings that let you manage who sees your posts, who can tag you, and even who can comment. Take time to explore these settings, making adjustments that feel right for your comfort level. It's like putting locks on your doors and deciding who gets a key.

Safe Browsing Practices. Safe browsing is akin to knowing which neighborhoods are safe to walk through at night. Here are some pointers:

- **Look for the 'lock' icon next to the website address. It indicates a secure connection.**

- **Be wary of clicking on links in emails or messages, especially if they seem out of character or too good to be true. When in doubt, go directly to the source by typing the URL into your browser.**

- **Update your software and apps regularly. Patches and updates often include fixes for security vulnerabilities.**

- **Consider using a Virtual Private Network (VPN), especially on public Wi-Fi. It creates a private tunnel for your data, keeping it from prying eyes.**

Visual Element: Cyber Safety Checklist. A brightly colored infographic that serves as a quick reference guide for staying safe online. It includes icons for solid passwords, privacy settings, secure browsing, and spotting scams, each accompanied by a brief, actionable tip. This visual can be pinned on bulletin boards, saved on phones, or shared on social media, constantly reminding us of the simple steps to protect our digital selves.

Interactive Element: Privacy Settings Walkthrough. An interactive guide that leads you step-by-step through the process of securing your social media profiles. It covers the major platforms and offers customizable advice depending on your privacy preferences. By answering a series of questions about who you want to see your posts, who can send you friend requests, and more, you'll receive a personalized set of recommendations to enhance your online privacy.

Textual Element: Real-Life Cyber Scam Examples. This compilation of real-life stories detailing common cyber scams and how they were spotted and avoided. Each story highlights the warning signs that something was amiss, such as unusual requests for information, misspelled URLs, or offers that seemed too good to be true. These narratives provide practical insights into cyber-criminals' tactics and emphasize the importance of vigilance and skepticism when navigating the digital world.

Navigating the bustling streets of our digital city with confidence comes down to being informed, alert, and prepared. By understanding the risks, securing our information with strong passwords, adjusting our privacy settings, and adopting safe browsing practices, we can enjoy the vast, interconnected world of the internet while keeping our digital treasures safe. Just as we lock our doors at night and avoid dark alleys, taking these precautions in the digital realm protects us and our personal information from those who wish to harm us.

The Impact of Social Media on Mental Health: Finding Balance. In the digital age, social media platforms have become the town squares and coffee shops of yesteryear, places where people gather to share, connect, and learn from one another. Yet, as we scroll through these virtual spaces, it's not uncommon to feel a tug on our self-esteem or sense of well-being. This section illuminates social media's impact on mental health, focusing on preserving self-esteem, managing screen time, finding positive communities, and valuing real-life connections.

Social Media and Self-Esteem. The curated perfection often showcased on social media can lead to unfair comparisons, with users measuring their everyday lives against the highlight reels of others. This discrepancy can chip away at self-esteem and distort body image, leaving individuals feeling inadequate or less successful. Remember that social media is a stage where people can present an idealized version of their lives, not the whole story. Cultivating a healthy perspective involves:

- **Reality Checks:** Remember that posts often show the best moments, not the daily struggles.

- **Diverse Follows:** Curate your feed to include accounts celebrating natural bodies, achievements, and challenges, enhancing your exposure to diverse and relatable content.

- **Positive Affirmations**: Engage in self-talk that reinforces your worth and achievements, independent of online validation.

Managing Screen Time. The allure of endless content can lead to hours lost in the digital scroll, contributing to digital burnout, where online engagement stops being enjoyable and starts feeling like a drain on energy and mood. Setting boundaries on screen time is akin to choosing a healthy diet; it's about balance. Strategies for managing screen time include:

- **Scheduled Breaks:** Allocate specific times during the day to check social media and stick to them. This limits impulsive scrolling and frees up time for other activities.

- **Tech-Free Zones**: Establish areas in your home, like the bedroom or dining table, where devices are off-limits. This will encourage in-person interactions and better sleep hygiene.

- **Mindful Scrolling:** Be intentional with your time online. Ask yourself whether your current activity is serving you positively or if it is time to log off and recharge offline.

Positive Online Communities. While social media can be a source of stress, it also has the potential to offer support, inspiration, and a sense of belonging. Finding and engaging with positive online communities can enhance your digital experience, providing a platform for shared interests, mutual support, and uplifting content. To connect with these communities:

- **Seek Interest-Based Groups:** Look for groups or pages focusing on your hobbies, passions, or support needs. These spaces are often more positive and focused than general social media feeds.

- **Contribute Positively:** When you find a community you resonate with, contribute constructively. Share your experiences, offer support, and celebrate others' achievements.

- **Set Notifications:** If a particular group or page consistently uplifts you, consider setting notifications so you don't miss their content amid the broader social media noise.

Real-Life Connections. In the whirlwind of likes, shares, and comments, it's easy to forget the value of face-to-face interactions. Real-life connections—those moments spent with family, friends, or even acquaintances in your community—provide a depth of emotional support and understanding that digital interactions struggle to replicate. To ensure these connections remain a cornerstone of your social life:

- **Schedule Regular Meetups:** Whether it's a weekly coffee with a friend or a family dinner, having these events on your calendar ensures you prioritize them.

- **Digital Detoxes:** Consider taking short breaks from social media, whether for a day or a weekend, to reconnect with the world around you and engage in activities that bring you joy.

- **Volunteer or Join Local Clubs:** Engaging in community service or joining clubs that align with your interests can expand your social circle and provide fulfilling, real-world interactions.

Navigating the digital landscape requires awareness and intention to guard against the potential pitfalls that social media can present to our mental health. By fostering a balanced perspective on social media's role in our lives, seeking out positive online spaces, setting boundaries around our digital consumption, and nurturing our real-world relationships, we can enjoy the benefits of connectivity without compromising our well-being.

To Post or Not to Post: Making Wise Decisions Online. In the digital age, every click, share, and post becomes a part of your online tapestry. This section unravels the complexities of digital sharing, guiding you through the thought process behind posting online, understanding the lasting impact of digital content, respecting digital consent, and navigating online disagreements with dignity and respect.

Thinking Before Posting. Every time you're about to share something online, it's like standing at a crossroads. One path leads to sharing without a second thought, while the other invites you to pause and consider the ramifications. Opting for the latter can save you from potential pitfalls. Here's what to ponder:

- **Is this necessary? Assess the value of your post. Does it contribute positively to your digital space, or could it be misunderstood or potentially regrettable?**

- **Who is my audience? Remember, what you share often reaches beyond your immediate circle. Future employers, college admissions officers, and even unknown online users could interpret your content in ways you didn't intend.**

- **Am I comfortable with this being permanent? The internet has a long memory. Copies might linger in screenshots or caches even if you delete a post.**

Future Implications. The digital footprints we leave today can shadow us into the future. Colleges and employers increasingly glance at social media profiles as part of their evaluation process. A spur-of-the-moment post can, unfortunately, become a stumbling block down the road. Here's how your digital presence can impact your future:

- **College Admissions:** Admissions officers may examine applicants' social media profiles to assess their character. Posts that reflect poorly on your judgment can be red flags.

- **Job Opportunities:** Many employers conduct online searches for potential hires. Content that suggests irresponsible behavior or poor communication skills can diminish your professional appeal.

- **Personal Relationships:** Future friendships and relationships can also be influenced by what others learn about you online.

Digital Consent. Just as we seek permission before borrowing a friend's belongings, digital consent involves asking before sharing content that affects others. This respect for privacy extends to photos, videos, and sensitive information. Here's how to practice digital consent:

- **Always Ask First: Get their approval before posting pictures or information involving others. What might seem harmless to you could be uncomfortable or invasive to someone else.**

- **Respect Boundaries: If someone asks not to be posted about or tagged, honor their request without question. Personal boundaries should be respected** both offline and online.

- **Consider the Impact: Reflect on how sharing certain information could affect the individuals involved. Could it embarrass or harm them now or in the future?**

Handling Online Disagreements. The cloak of anonymity and the distance the internet provides can sometimes lead to heated exchanges. However, maintaining decorum and respect during online disagreements is crucial. Here's how to keep things civil:

- **Pause Before Responding:** Giving yourself time to cool down can prevent you from saying something you might regret. Construct your responses with care, aiming for dialogue, not conflict.

- **Agree to Disagree:** Not every debate needs a winner. Sometimes, it's best to agree to disagree and move on respectfully.

- **Avoid Personal Attacks:** Keep the discussion focused on ideas rather than resorting to personal attacks. Insults and derogatory comments only worsen the situation and poorly reflect your character.

- **Seek Private Resolutions:** If a public exchange is going nowhere, consider moving the discussion to a private message or, better yet, resolving the disagreement offline.

Our online actions and decisions shape our digital identity and influence real-world opportunities and relationships in this digital era. Being mindful of what we share, understanding the potential long-term consequences of our online content, practicing digital consent, and handling online disagreements with respect are crucial steps in navigating the complex web of digital interactions. These practices safeguard our digital well-being and ensure our online presence reflects our best selves.

Digital Footprint: How Your Online Activity Can Affect Your Future. In today's interconnected world, the digital trails we leave are more like highways than footpaths. Every like, share, comment, and post contributes to a digital footprint that can span the vast expanse of the internet. This imprint we leave behind isn't just fleeting steps in digital sand; it's a lasting marker of our online presence, visible to friends, family, potential employers, and even strangers. Understanding the nature and impact of our digital footprints is the first step in navigating the online world with confidence and caution.

Understanding Digital Footprints. A digital footprint is essentially the record of your interactions in the digital environment. This includes the websites you visit, the social media content you post, and even the comments you leave on various platforms. Some of these footprints are passive, such as data gathered from browsing habits by cookies. Others are active, the result of deliberate interactions with digital content. Both types contribute to a profile of who you are online, which can have implications far beyond the moment of a single post or click.

Curating a Positive Online Image. Creating a positive online presence is akin to curating an art exhibit of your life where you have control over how you're perceived. Here's how you can ensure that your digital footprint reflects your true self:

- **Be Mindful of Content:** Before posting anything, consider if it's something you'd be comfortable with everyone seeing, from a close friend to a future employer. If there's any doubt, it might be best left unshared.

- **Showcase Achievements:** Don't shy away from sharing your accomplishments, be they academic, artistic, or personal growth milestones. These positive posts contribute to a digital footprint that speaks to your strengths and character.

- **Positive Interaction:** Engage with others online in a constructive manner. Supportive comments, insightful discussions, and shared interests can all paint a picture of a thoughtful and kind individual.

Regular Online Audits. Just as businesses regularly take inventory, conducting personal audits of your online presence can help keep your digital footprint aligned with how you wish to be seen. Here's a straightforward approach:

- **Google Yourself:** Start with a simple search of your name in various search engines. This can reveal what others see when they look you up online.

- **Check Privacy Settings:** Regularly review the privacy settings on all your social media accounts to control who sees what you post.

- **Evaluate Your Content:** Scroll through your profiles and take note of anything that doesn't **represent who**

you are or how you want to be perceived.

Deleting and Managing Old Content. Our opinions, interests, and even our sense of humor can change as we grow. Old posts may no longer reflect who you are today. Here's how to manage content that's no longer representative:

- **Delete With Care:** If a post no longer represents you or could be misunderstood, consider deleting it. Remember, once something is online, it can be challenging to remove it entirely.

- **Archive When Possible:** Some platforms allow you to archive posts, removing them from public view without permanently deleting them. This can be a good option for content you're unsure about.

- **Update Regularly:** As your interests and achievements evolve, so should your online profiles. Regular updates ensure your digital footprint keeps pace with your real-life growth.

In essence, your digital footprint is the sum of your interactions in the online world, a lasting record that can influence your future in unforeseen ways. By understanding the nature of digital footprints, actively curating a positive online image, conducting regular audits of your online presence, and thoughtfully managing old content, you can ensure that your digital footprint is an accurate and flattering reflection of who you are. In doing so, you navigate the digital world cautiously but confidently, aware of the impact your online activity can have on your future.

Combating Cyberbullying: Strategies for Teens and Their Parents

The digital world, much like the physical one, has its dark alleys and hidden corners where negativity thrives, often manifesting as cyberbullying. This form of harassment can leave lasting scars, making it crucial for both teens and their parents to understand how to confront and overcome it.

Recognizing Cyberbullying. Cyberbullying can be more insidious than its offline counterpart, hiding behind screens and anonymous profiles. It's vital to spot the signs early. These may include receiving hurtful messages, being the subject of rumors spread online, or experiencing exclusion from online groups. The impact on one's mental health can be profound, leading to feelings of isolation, depression, and anxiety. Recognizing these signs in oneself and friends can be the first step toward addressing the issue.

Responding to Cyberbullying. Reacting to cyberbullying requires both resilience and strategy. Here are some steps to consider:

- **Do Not Retaliate: Responding with anger can escalate the situation. It's better to take a step back and approach the problem calmly.**

- **Document Everything: Keep records of bullying messages, posts, or comments. These can serve as evidence if the situation needs to be escalated.**

- **Report the Abuse: Most social media platforms have mechanisms for reporting harassment. Use these tools to report cyberbullies and have their content reviewed and potentially removed.**

- **Block the Offenders: Don't hesitate to block individuals harassing you. This can provide immediate relief from the situation.**

Support Systems. Having a network of support is essential when dealing with cyberbullying. This network can include:

- **Parents:** Open communication with your parents can provide emotional support and practical advice on handling the situation.

- **Teachers and School Counselors:** Schools often have protocols for dealing with cyberbullying. Informing a trusted teacher or counselor can initiate these support mechanisms.

- **Friends:** Friends can offer immediate emotional support and help stand up to online and offline bullies.

Creating a dialogue about cyberbullying within these support systems can foster an environment where teens feel safe to share their experiences and seek help.

Creating a Positive Digital Culture. Promoting a culture of kindness and respect online is everyone's responsibility. Here are ways teens can contribute to a healthier digital environment:

- **Be a Digital Ally: Stand up for others bullied online. Showing your support can make a big difference to someone feeling isolated.**

- **Promote Positive Content: Share and create content that uplifts and encourages others. Positive posts can**

counterbalance negativity and spread kindness.

- **Educate Peers: Encourage discussions about the impact of cyberbullying and the importance of positive online interactions among your friends and peers.**

By actively working towards a more positive digital culture, teens combat cyberbullying and contribute to creating a safer online community for everyone. In navigating the complex web of digital interactions, they understand the shadowy corners where cyberbullying lurks, which is crucial. Recognizing the signs, knowing how to respond effectively, leveraging support systems, and actively fostering a culture of positivity and respect are critical strategies in combating this issue. These actions help deal with cyberbullying when it occurs and prevent it from spreading, ensuring the digital world remains a space for connection, learning, and growth.

As we move forward, let's carry with us the understanding that our online actions and words have power. They can either contribute to a cycle of negativity or help build a supportive and positive digital environment. The choice is ours to make, and it's a choice that can shape not just our own online experiences but those of others around us. In the next chapter, we'll explore another crucial aspect of our digital lives, focusing on how we can use technology safely, responsibly, and creatively to enrich our lives and the lives of others.

Chapter Seven

Financial Literacy for Teens

I magine your bank account as a personal treasure chest, where every coin and bill saved is a testament to your hard work, intelligent decisions, and future dreams. Yet, without the map of financial literacy, navigating the seas of personal finance can feel overwhelming, leaving that chest less filled than it could be. This chapter sails into budgeting basics, showing you how to manage your money like a pro, ensuring your treasure chest grows with every wise choice.

Budgeting Basics: Managing Your Money Like a Pro

Understanding Your Cash Flow. Cash flow is the movement of money in and out of your wallet or bank account. It's like watching the tide; sometimes, it's high, and other times, it's low. It is crucial to keep an eye on this tide—knowing where your money comes from (income) and where it goes (expenses). Start by tracking your money for a month. Note every dollar earned from part-time jobs, allowances, or gifts and every dollar spent on movies, snacks, or savings for that new phone. This snapshot gives you a clear picture of your financial health and is the first step toward taking control of your finances.

Creating a Budget. Think of a budget as your personal finance blueprint. It's a plan for spending and saving money based on your goals and cash flow. Here's how to create one:

- **List Your Income:** Write down all sources of money you receive regularly.

- **Track Your Expenses:** Categorize them into needs (like food and transport) and wants (like entertainment).

- **Set Goals:** Determine what you're saving for, be it college, a car, or a concert ticket.

- **Allocate Funds:** Decide how much money goes where based on your income and goals.

Sticking to this plan ensures you cover your needs and work towards your wants without breaking the bank.

Budgeting Tools. Several apps and tools can simplify tracking your cash flow and sticking to your budget. Apps like Mint and You Need A Budget (YNAB) link to your bank accounts, categorize your expenses automatically and even set savings goals. For those who prefer a more hands-on approach, spreadsheet templates in Excel or Google Sheets offer complete customization of your budgeting system. These tools do the heavy lifting, turning the daunting task of budgeting into a manageable, even enjoyable, part of your routine.

Sticking to Your Budget

Adhering to your budget, especially when faced with temptations, is where the real challenge lies. Here are strategies to keep you on track:

- **Prioritize Your Goals:** Remind yourself of what you're saving for. Visualize the satisfaction of reaching that goal.

- **Envelope System:** For variable expenses like dining out, use envelopes to allocate a set amount of cash for the month. Once it's gone, that's it until next month.

- **Track Your Spending:** Regularly review where your money is going. Apps can send alerts when you're close to exceeding your budget in a category.

- **Reward Yourself:** Set aside a small part of your budget for treats. Staying disciplined doesn't mean you can't enjoy your money.

Budgeting Challenge. This is an interactive, month-long budgeting challenge in which you track your spending and try to stick to your budget using one of the recommended tools. Weekly prompts encourage reflection on your spending habits and adjustments to your budget and celebrate your successes. This hands-on experience reinforces the budgeting habit and makes the learning process dynamic and engaging. By mastering the basics of budgeting, you're laying the foundation for a financially secure future. Understanding your cash flow, creating a realistic budget, utilizing modern tools to keep track of your finances, and developing strategies to stick to your budget are all essential skills in managing your money effectively. With these skills in your arsenal, your treasure chest is bound to grow, funding your current needs and future dreams.

The Truth About Credit: What Teens Need to Know. Navigating the world of credit is akin to learning a new language, filled with its vocabulary and rules. Understanding this language is crucial for financial health, as credit plays a pivotal role in many of life's significant milestones, from buying a car to owning a home. Here, we decode the essentials of credit, highlighting the importance of building good credit, using it wisely and steering clear of pitfalls that could harm your financial future.

Credit Basics. At its core, credit is the ability to borrow money with the promise to pay it back later, often with interest. This concept is central to various forms of borrowing, including credit cards and loans. Two key terms in the credit world are credit scores and interest rates.

- **Credit Scores:** A numerical expression based on an analysis of your credit files, representing the creditworthiness of an individual. Think of it as a financial grade, with scores ranging from 300 to 850. Higher scores make borrowing cheaper, as they indicate to lenders that you're a low-risk borrower.

- **Interest Rates:** The cost of borrowing money is typically expressed as a percentage of the borrowed amount. This rate can vary widely based on the type of credit, the lender, and your credit score.

Understanding these basics sets the stage for using credit to your advantage, allowing you to make informed decisions about borrowing and repayment strategies.

The Importance of Good Credit. Good credit isn't just a number; it's a gateway to financial opportunities. A strong credit score can improve loan terms, lower insurance premiums, and influence job prospects. Conversely, a low score can limit your borrowing options, making loans more expensive or out of reach. Building good credit involves several practices, such as paying bills on time, keeping debt levels low, and only applying for new credit when necessary. It's a slow process, but the payoff is substantial: It gives you leverage in negotiations and saves you money in the long run.

Using Credit Responsibly. Credit cards and loans are tools, not free money. Using these tools responsibly is critical to maintaining good credit. Here are some best practices:

- **Pay on Time:** Late payments can significantly impact your credit score. Setting up automatic payments or reminders ensures you get all the due dates.

- **Understand the Terms:** Before signing up for a credit card or accepting a loan, fully understand the terms, including interest rates, fees, and repayment schedules.

- **Keep Balances Low:** High balances relative to your credit limit can hurt your score. Aim to keep balances below 30% of your available credit.

- **Monitor Your Credit:** Regularly check your credit report for errors or unauthorized activity. You're entitled to one free annual report from the three major credit bureaus.

Adopting these habits helps build and maintain a healthy credit profile, benefiting your financial life.

Avoiding Debt Traps. Credit can be a double-edged sword, offering financial flexibility and leading to debt if not managed carefully. Debt traps are a real risk, where borrowing leads to a cycle of debt that is challenging to escape. Common traps include:

- **Only Paying the Minimum:** Paying only the minimum due on credit cards keeps you in debt longer, increasing the amount paid due to interest.

- **Taking on Too Much Debt:** Borrowing more than you can afford to repay can lead to missed payments and a spiraling debt cycle.

- **Payday Loans:** These short-term, high-interest loans can seem like a quick fix but often lead to long-term debt due to their steep interest rates and fees.

Awareness and self-discipline are your best defenses against these traps. Stick to a budget, borrow only what you need, and always have a repayment plan.

Navigating the credit landscape requires a solid understanding of its fundamentals, a commitment to responsible usage, and vigilance against potential pitfalls. With this knowledge, you can use credit to your advantage, opening doors to financial opportunities and securing a stable financial future.

Saving for the Future: Why It's Never Too Early to Start. Saving money might not seem as thrilling as spending it but think of savings as the seeds you plant today that grow into the financial security and freedom you'll enjoy tomorrow. It's about making the future you say, "Thank you!" Whether aiming for a new game console next month or eyeing college expenses, setting aside some of your money now ensures you can reach those goals without unnecessary stress or debt.

Setting Financial Goals. Goals give your savings journey direction and purpose. They can range from short-term objectives, like buying concert tickets or new sneakers, to long-term ambitions, such as funding higher education or even starting a business. When setting these goals, specificity is your friend. Instead of saying, "I want to save for a car," determine the type of car, its cost, and when you hope to buy it. This clarity transforms vague wishes into attainable targets, making the process of saving not just more focused but also more motivating.

Savings Accounts and Options. Not all savings solutions are created equal, and choosing the right home for your money can significantly impact how much you save over time. Traditional savings accounts at banks are a reliable starting point, offering safety and some interest on your balance. However, for those willing to explore, other options like high-yield savings accounts or Certificates of Deposit (CDs) often provide higher interest rates, helping your savings grow faster. If you're looking ahead and want to start saving for retirement (it's never too early!), consider a Roth IRA. This account type allows your investments to grow tax-free, which can make a substantial difference over the decades.

- **Regular Savings Account:** Ideal for beginners and those looking for easy access to their funds.

- **High-Yield Savings Account:** High interest rates are perfect for medium-term goals.

- **Certificates of Deposit (CDs):** Locks in your money for a fixed term at a fixed rate, usually offering higher interest than savings accounts.

- **Roth IRA:** A retirement savings account that lets your investments grow tax-free, suitable for long-term goals.

The Power of Compound Interest. Compound interest is often hailed as one of the wonders of the financial world, and for good reason. It's where your money starts making money on its own. Here's a simple breakdown: when you save money in an interest-bearing account, you earn interest on your initial deposit. Over time, you start making interest on your original amount, and the interest has already accrued. This cycle continues, with your savings growing exponentially, rather than linearly, over time. To see the true magic of compound interest, start saving as early as possible—the longer your money grows, the more you will benefit from this financial phenomenon.

Saving Strategies. Consistency is vital when it comes to building your savings. Here are some strategies to help make saving a regular part of your financial routine:

- **Automate Your Savings:** Many banks offer the option to automatically transfer a portion of your paycheck into a savings account. This "set it and forget it" method ensures you consistently save without thinking about it each month.

- **Save Any Windfalls:** Did you get birthday money or earn a bonus from a part-time job? Please resist the urge to spend it all and allocate a portion to your savings. These unexpected boosts can help you reach your goals faster.

- **Challenge Yourself:** Engage in savings challenges, like the 52-week challenge, where you save an increasing amount of money each week for a year. It starts quickly but adds up to a significant sum by the end.

- **Track Your Progress:** Monitor your growing savings. Seeing the numbers climb can be incredibly rewarding and motivates you to keep going.

Incorporating these saving strategies into your life builds your financial nest egg and instills habits that will benefit you. These steps are crucial in securing your financial future, from setting clear goals and understanding the different saving options available to harnessing the power of compound interest and sticking to a saving plan. Start today and watch how even small amounts can grow, proving there's no time like the present for saving.

Making Money: Ideas for Teen Entrepreneurs and Part-Time Jobs. In today's dynamic world, teens like you have myriad opportunities to save and earn money, paving the way for financial independence and a deeper understanding of the value of hard-earned cash. From exploring part-time job options to diving into entrepreneurship and freelancing, let's look at how you can start filling your treasure chest today.

Part-Time Job Opportunities. Securing a part-time job is a tried-and-true method for teens to earn money. Not only does it provide a steady income, but it also imparts crucial life skills such as time management, responsibility, and teamwork. However, balancing school, homework, and extracurriculars with work hours can be challenging. Here's what to consider:

- **Flexibility is Key:** Look for jobs that accommodate your school schedule. Many local businesses, understanding the demands placed on students, are willing to offer flexible hours.

- **Build Your Skillset:** Choose positions that offer more than just a paycheck. Jobs that enhance your communication, customer service, or technical skills can greatly benefit your future career.

- **Know Your Rights:** Familiarize yourself with labor laws regarding teen employment in your area. This knowledge ensures you know the number of hours you're allowed to work and the minimum wage you should receive.

Entrepreneurial Ventures. Starting a small business could be perfect for those who dream of being their own boss. Teen entrepreneurship is on the rise, thanks to the accessibility of online platforms and social media. Here are some ideas to get you started:

- **Customized Merchandise:** With platforms like Etsy or Redbubble, you can sell art, customized clothing, or handmade jewelry. This avenue allows you to turn your hobbies into a profitable business.

- **Tech Services:** If you're tech-savvy, offer your services for website design, app development, or tech support. Many small businesses and individuals need affordable tech assistance.

- **Tutoring or Teaching:** Do you excel at a subject, instrument, or sport? Offer your expertise as a tutor or coach. This not only earns you money but also reinforces your skills.

Freelancing and Gigs. The gig economy offers flexibility and variety, allowing you to work on projects matching your skills and interests. Websites like Fiverr and Upwork connect freelancers with clients needing services ranging from graphic design to writing to digital marketing. Here's how to thrive in the gig economy:

- **Showcase Your Skills:** Create a compelling profile highlighting your skills, experience, and relevant projects or coursework. A strong portfolio can set you apart from the competition.

- **Start Small:** To build your reputation, you might have to initially take on smaller projects or charge lower rates. Positive reviews from these early gigs can lead to more lucrative opportunities.

- **Manage Your Time Wisely:** Freelancing requires self-discipline. Set a schedule to meet client deadlines without compromising your schoolwork or personal time.

Financial Management for Young Entrepreneurs. Earning your own money is exhilarating, but managing it wisely is where the real challenge lies. Here are tips for young entrepreneurs and part-timers to keep their finances in check:

- **Track Your Earnings and Expenses:** Use a simple spreadsheet or a budgeting app to monitor how much you're making and where it's going. This visibility is crucial for making informed financial decisions.

- **Set Aside Money for Taxes:** If you're freelancing or running your own business, you'll likely need to pay taxes on your income. Regularly setting aside a portion of your earnings can prevent tax-time surprises.

- **Reinvest in Your Business:** Consider using some of your earnings to grow your venture, whether by purchasing better equipment, investing in marketing, or taking a course to enhance your skills.

- **Save for the Future:** Remember to allocate some of your income to your savings goals. Remember, every dollar saved today is a step closer to financial independence.

In this rapidly changing economy, teens have more opportunities than ever to earn money in ways that align with their interests, skills, and schedules. Whether you opt for a part-time job, dive into entrepreneurship, or explore freelancing, the key is to start. With each paycheck, sale, or completed project, you're earning money, building invaluable skills, gaining experience, and laying the groundwork for a financially secure future.

Navigating the World of Student Loans: A Primer for College-Bound Teens

Paying for college is a significant milestone that comes with challenges and decisions, notably around student loans. While these loans can be valuable in bridging the gap between savings and college expenses, understanding how they operate is crucial to making informed choices and avoiding common pitfalls.

Understanding Student Loans. At its most basic, a student loan is money borrowed to pay for higher education, which must be paid back with interest. Loans can cover tuition, room and board, books, and other education-related expenses. Distinguishing between the principal amount (the initial sum borrowed) and the interest (the cost of borrowing that money) is critical. Interest rates and repayment terms can vary, affecting the total amount you'll pay back over time.

Federal vs. Private Loans. The distinction between federal and private student loans is critical. Federal loans, backed by the government, often come with lower interest rates and more flexible repayment options than private loans from banks or other financial institutions. Federal loans also offer features like income-driven repayment plans and potential loan forgiveness programs. On the other hand, private loans may require a co-signer and typically have less lenient terms for repayment. Here's a quick comparison:

- **Federal Loans:** Lower fixed interest rates, income-driven repayment plans, deferment, and forbearance options.

- **Private Loans:** Higher or variable interest rates and stricter repayment conditions typically require a credit check.

Applying for Financial Aid and Scholarships. Before diving into loans, explore financial aid and scholarships. The Free Application for Federal Student Aid (FAFSA) is your gateway to federal grants, loans, and work-study funds. Filling out the FAFSA should be your first step, as it can provide access to need-based financial aid that doesn't need to be repaid. Scholarships, another form of aid that doesn't require repayment, are available from various sources—colleges, companies, non-profits, and community organizations. Here's how to maximize your chances:

- **Apply Early:** Many scholarships and grant programs have limited funds. The sooner you apply, the better your chances.

- **Search Widely:** Use scholarship search engines and check with your high school counselors for opportunities that match your background, interests, and academic goals.

- **Tailor Your Applications:** Customize your applications to fit the scholarship criteria, focusing on how your experiences and aspirations align with their objectives.

Loan Repayment Strategies. Once you graduate, repaying your student loans becomes a new chapter in your financial life. Here are strategies to manage and repay your loans effectively:

- **Understand Your Repayment Plan:** Familiarize yourself with your repayment schedule, monthly payment amount, and loan interest rate.

- **Consider Consolidation or Refinancing:** If you have

multiple loans, consolidating them into a single loan can simplify repayment. Refinancing at a lower interest rate can reduce monthly payments, though this option is more familiar with private loans.

- **Explore Forgiveness and Repayment Programs:** For federal loans, programs like Public Service Loan Forgiveness (PSLF) offer loan forgiveness after making 120 qualifying payments while working in public service. Income-driven repayment plans adjust your monthly payments based on income and family size.

- **Stay on Top of Payments:** It's crucial to avoid late payments or default. Contact your loan servicer to discuss deferment or forbearance options if you're facing financial difficulties.

Student loans may seem daunting as you move closer to college, but they're a manageable and often necessary part of many students' higher education financing plans. By understanding how loans work, the differences between federal and private options, maximizing scholarships and grants, and developing a solid repayment plan, you can invest in your education confidently, knowing you're equipped to handle the financial responsibility that comes with it.

In wrapping up, navigating the financial aspects of higher education demands attention, research, and strategic planning. The knowledge gained from understanding student loans and pursuing scholarships and grants lays a strong foundation for making informed decisions about financing your college education. As we transition from this exploration of financial literacy into the next chapter, remember that each financial decision you make, big or small, shapes your path toward independence and success in the years to come.

Chapter Eight
Practical Life Skills

I magine waking up to the aroma of freshly baked muffins, which reminds you of weekend mornings at home. Now, picture being able to recreate that memory right in your kitchen, not just because you want to, but because you know how. This chapter isn't just about recipes; it's about fostering independence, nurturing well-being, and turning necessity into self-expression. It's about transforming the mundane task of feeding oneself into an opportunity for creativity, connection, and care.

Cooking is a fundamental life skill, yet for many teens, the kitchen remains uncharted territory, a place visited only out of necessity. Here, we shift that narrative. From basic cooking techniques to simple, healthy recipes, meal planning, and kitchen safety, this chapter equips you with the knowledge to navigate the kitchen confidently, efficiently, and safely.

Basic Cooking Techniques. Cooking might seem daunting initially, but like any skill, it becomes more manageable once you break it down. Here are a few techniques that every teen should master:

- **Boiling and simmering are perfect for pasta, veggies, and soups.** The key difference? Boiling involves cooking food in bubbling water while simmering involves cooking food at a lower temperature, where the water barely bubbles.

- **Sautéing:** Ideal for quick meals. All you need is a pan, some oil, and your ingredients. It's fast and easy and preserves the flavors.

- **Baking:** Not just for desserts. Baking can be a hands-off method for making delicious and nutritious meals with minimal effort.

- **Grilling:** Great for meats and veggies, grilling adds a smoky flavor and can be a healthier cooking method since it allows fat to drip away from the food.

Simple and Healthy Recipes. Time and budget constraints are real, but so is the need for nutritious meals. Here are a few recipes that tick all the boxes:

- **Overnight oats:** Mix oats with milk or a dairy-free alternative, add some chia seeds and a dash of maple syrup, and leave it in the fridge overnight. Top with fresh fruits in the morning for a quick, healthy breakfast.

- **Stir-fry:** This is a versatile option. Grab veggies and some protein (chicken, tofu, beef) and toss them in a pan with oil and soy sauce. Serve over rice or noodles.

- **Sheet pan meals:** Toss chopped veggies and a protein source with olive oil and your favorite seasonings on a baking sheet. Bake until everything's cooked through. It's that easy.

Meal Planning and Prep. Meal planning saves time, money, and stress. Start by deciding what you want to eat for the week. Make a shopping list to avoid buying things you don't need. Dedicate a few hours over the weekend to prep parts of your meals ahead of time. Chop veggies, cook grains, or even make whole dishes that can be easily reheated. This way, you're starting from scratch only some days.

Kitchen Safety. Safety in the kitchen is non-negotiable. Here are some essential tips:

- **Never leave cooking food unattended:** A leading cause of kitchen fires.

- **Keep your workspace clean:** Wash your hands thoroughly before and after handling food.

- **Learn how to use a knife properly:** Dull knives are more dangerous than sharp ones because they require more cutting force.

- **Understand how to extinguish a grease fire:** Water worsens it. Instead, smother the flames with a lid or use baking soda.

Cooking is more than just a means to an end; it's a way to take care of yourself and others, to explore new flavors and cultures, and to express creativity. By mastering these essential cooking skills, you're not just preparing meals; you're preparing for life. With each dish you make, you're one step closer to making that kitchen your own, transforming it from a place of necessity to a space of possibility.

Laundry Lessons: From Sorting to Folding. Doing laundry is more than just a chore; it's a skill that, once learned, can significantly change how you present yourself to the world. Neat, clean clothes say a lot about a person, and knowing how to care for them properly ensures they last longer and look better. Let's break down the process, from sorting your laundry to folding it neatly for your closet.

Sorting Laundry. Sorting isn't just about separating lights from darks. It's a crucial step that protects your clothes and ensures they get the cleanliness they need without damage. Here are the basics:

- **By Color:** Separate whites, lights, and darks to prevent colors from bleeding.

- **By Fabric Type:** Wash delicate fabrics separately from heavier ones like jeans or towels to avoid damage.

- **By Washing Instructions:** Check labels for special care instructions. Some items may need a gentler cycle or a different temperature.

Sorting correctly might take a few extra minutes, but keeping your wardrobe in shape is worth it.

Washing and Drying Basics. Washing machines and dryers might seem intimidating with all their settings, but they're pretty straightforward once you get the hang of them. Here's what you need to know:

- **Reading Labels:** Before anything else, read the care labels on your clothes. They'll tell you the water temperature to use, which cycle is best, and whether an item can be tumble-dried.

- **Choosing the Right Detergent:** Many types of detergent include regular, high-efficiency pods and powders. Again, labels are your friends here. Some fabrics require specific detergents.

- **Setting the Machine:** A regular cycle with cold water is fine for most loads and saves energy. Use warm or hot water for heavily soiled clothes or to ensure sanitization (like for bed linens or bath towels).

- **Drying:** Only some things should go in the dryer. Hang delicate items or those prone to shrinking. For the rest, use a low or medium heat setting to prevent damage and save energy.

Understanding your machines and how to use them can transform laundry from a task you dread to just another part of your routine.

Ironing and Folding. Ironing and folding might seem like the final, optional steps, but they make your clothes look crisp and store neatly. Here's how to do it right:

- **Ironing:** Always check the label for the correct temperature setting. Iron in long, straight strokes; use steam or a water spray for stubborn wrinkles. Use an ironing board for the best results, and start with items requiring the lowest temperature, moving to those needing higher heat.

- **Folding:** To minimize wrinkles, the key to folding is immediately after drying. Shirts can be folded down the middle and into thirds, while pants can be folded in half and then over once or twice, depending on length. Rolling instead of folding is a good option for items that wrinkle easily.

Properly ironed and folded clothes look better and are easier to store and find in your closet or drawers.

Dealing with Stains. Stains are inevitable, but they don't have to be permanent. Here's how to tackle them:

- **Act Fast:** The sooner you address a stain, the better your chances of removing it.

- **Blot, Don't Rub:** Gently blot a stain with a clean cloth or paper towel to prevent it from spreading.

- **Use the Right Remover:** Different stains require different treatments. Grease stains, for example, can often be treated with dish soap, while ink might need rubbing alcohol.

- **Test First:** Before applying any treatment, test it on a small, inconspicuous area of the fabric to ensure it will not damage it.

With some know-how, most stains can be removed, saving your clothes from being relegated to your wardrobe's 'at-home only' section. Laundry doesn't have to be daunting. With these tips on sorting, washing, drying, ironing, folding, and stain removal, you'll master the art of laundry. Not only will your clothes thank you, but you'll also feel a sense of accomplishment knowing you can confidently tackle this essential life skill.

Basic Home Repairs: A Teen's DIY Guide. Navigating the ins and outs of home maintenance might seem like a daunting task reserved for adults. However, gaining a basic understanding of home repairs is not just about saving money on professionals; it's about developing self-reliance and the confidence to address problems head-on. This section explores the essentials every teen should know about handling simple home repairs and when seeking expert help is wise.

Toolbox Essentials. Before diving into any repair task, gathering the right tools is crucial. A well-equipped toolbox is your best ally, ensuring you're prepared for various maintenance tasks. Here are some must-haves:

- **Screwdrivers:** A set with various sizes and heads (flathead and Phillips) will come in handy for everything from tightening cabinet hinges to assembling furniture.

- **Adjustable Wrench:** An adjustable wrench can fit various nut and bolt sizes, making it ideal for plumbing tasks.

- **Hammer:** A versatile tool for hanging pictures or assembling items. A claw hammer also allows you to remove nails easily.

- **Pliers:** Locking, needle-nose, and adjustable pliers are great for gripping, bending, or cutting wire.

- **Tape Measure**: A tape measure is essential whether you're hanging shelves or simply measuring space for new furniture.

- **Level:** Ensures your DIY projects aren't just strong but also straight and well-aligned.

- **Utility Knife:** This is for cutting through packaging, trimming wallpaper, or scoring materials before cutting.

- **Flashlight:** Illuminates your work area, crucial for tasks in dimly lit spaces or during power outages.

Equipping yourself with these essential tools prepares you to tackle a variety of ordinary repairs and projects around the house.

Simple Repairs. With your toolbox ready, let's look at some basic repairs you can confidently handle:

- **Fixing a Leaky Faucet:** Often caused by a worn-out washer or O-ring, this repair can be as simple as shutting off the water supply, disassembling the faucet, and replacing the faulty part.

- **Unclogging Drains:** Try a plunger or a plumber's snake to dislodge clogs before reaching for harsh chemicals. Baking soda and vinegar can also be effective for minor blockages.

- **Patching Holes in Walls:** Small holes from nails or screws can be filled with spackling paste, smoothed out, and painted over once dry.

- **Tightening Loose Handles and Hinges:** A quick turn with a screwdriver can secure loose cabinet handles or door hinges, instantly making fixtures more functional. These repairs save a call to the handyman and instill a sense of achievement and independence.

Preventative Maintenance. Regular maintenance is critical to preventing minor issues from turning into big problems. Here are some preventive measures to keep your home in top shape:

- **Cleaning Gutters:** Removing leaves and debris from gutters prevents water damage to your home's foundation and roof.

- **Checking for Leaks:** Periodically inspect under sinks and around appliances for signs of leaks. Catching them early can prevent costly water damage.

- **Replacing Filters:** Regularly changing air filters in your HVAC system ensures it runs efficiently and maintains indoor air quality.

- **Sealing Gaps:** Caulking around windows and doors helps keep your home insulated, reducing energy bills.

These maintenance tasks prolong the life of your home's components and contribute to a healthier living environment.

When to Call a Professional. While many repairs are within your reach, recognizing when to call in a professional is equally important. Here are scenarios when expert help is warranted:

- **Electrical Work:** Electrical repairs can be dangerous and require a licensed electrician, beyond changing a lightbulb or resetting a tripped breaker.

- **Major Plumbing Issues:** If you're dealing with more than a simple clog or a leaky faucet, consult a plumber to avoid causing further damage.

- **Structural Changes:** Any work that involves altering the structure of your home should be handled by a professional to ensure it's done safely and up to code.

- **Gas Appliances:** Repairs involving gas lines or appliances should always be left to experts due to the risk of leaks and fires.

Understanding your limits and when to seek professional assistance ensures that repairs are done safely and correctly, protecting your home and well-being. Embarking on the journey of essential home repairs empowers you to take control of common household issues, providing a foundation of skills that will serve you well into adulthood. Whether tightening a loose screw or patching a hole in the wall, each task completed is a step toward becoming more self-sufficient and confident in your ability to maintain and improve your living space.

Time Management: Balancing School, Work, and Play. In the whirlwind of teenage life, where academics, part-time jobs, and personal interests collide, mastering time management is akin to finding the secret recipe for a well-lived day. It's about carving out moments for responsibilities and relaxation, ensuring neither overshadows the other. Once honed, this skill paves the way for academic success and career readiness and ensures ample space for joy and leisure.

Prioritizing Tasks. The art of prioritization lies in distinguishing between what must be done and what can wait. A helpful method here is the Eisenhower Matrix, which categorizes tasks into four quadrants based on urgency and importance. Urgent and vital tasks demand immediate attention, while essential but not urgent tasks are scheduled for later. Urgent but less important tasks might be delegated, and those neither critical nor necessary can often be set aside or eliminated. This method clarifies your daily to-dos, highlighting paths through your workload that optimize your time and energy for what truly matters.

- **Daily Reflection:** Spend a few minutes each evening evaluating tasks for the next day and putting them into the matrix to visualize priorities.

- **Flexibility:** While some tasks remain fixed, be ready to adjust your priorities as new tasks emerge or circumstances change.

Effective Scheduling. Creating a schedule that accommodates work, study, and downtime is not just about listing activities; it's about understanding the rhythm of your day and fitting tasks into slots where they naturally belong. Tools like digital calendars or planners are invaluable here, offering a visual layout of your day, week, or month.

- **Time Blocking:** Assign specific blocks of time to different activities or tasks. For instance, dedicate a block to homework immediately after school when your mind is still in 'work mode.'

- **Breaks Are Essential:** Intersperse blocks of focused work with short breaks. Techniques like the Pomodoro Technique—25 minutes of work followed by a 5-minute break—can boost productivity and prevent burnout.

- **Leave Room for the Unexpected:** Life is unpredictable. Allotting buffer times between tasks accounts for interruptions or tasks that take longer than anticipated.

Avoiding Procrastination. Procrastination, often a thief of time, can be countered with strategies that tackle the issue's root—avoidance, feeling overwhelmed, or lacking motivation.

- **Break Tasks Down:** Large projects can seem daunting. Breaking them into smaller, manageable parts makes them less intimidating and more accessible to start.

- **Set Mini-Deadlines:** Set a deadline for each small task or part of a larger project. These mini milestones can create a sense of urgency and accomplishment.

- **Find Your Motivators:** Rewards can be powerful motivators. Allow yourself a treat or leisure activity after completing a task or reaching a milestone.

- **Change Your Environment:** A shift in surroundings can boost focus and productivity. If your usual study spot becomes associated with procrastination, find a new one.

Work-Life Balance. Achieving balance ensures that dedication to school and work doesn't eclipse the time spent on personal growth, relationships, and relaxation. This balance is crucial for mental and emotional well-being.

- **Set Boundaries:** Clearly define when and where school or work ends and personal time begins. Communicate these boundaries to friends, family, and employers.

- **Quality Over Quantity:** Make the moments spent on leisure count. Engage fully in activities you enjoy, whether reading, sports, or spending time with loved ones.

- **Self-Care:** Schedule activities that promote well-being regularly. Exercise, meditation, hobbies, and social outings contribute to a well-rounded life.

- **Reflect and Adjust:** Regularly assess how well your current schedule serves your needs for balance. Be prepared to adjust to better align with your goals for achievement and relaxation.

Effective time management emerges as a critical skill when navigating the complex landscape of adolescence, where educational, professional, and personal spheres intersect. It enables you to meet academic and work commitments with excellence while ensuring that pursuing passions and enjoying life's simpler pleasures are not sidelined. With prioritization, thoughtful scheduling, strategies to keep procrastination at bay, and a commitment to maintaining a healthy work-life balance, you are well-equipped to navigate the demands of teenage years with grace and success.

The Ultimate Guide to Public Transportation. Getting around town only sometimes requires a personal vehicle, especially when public transit options abound. For many teens, learning to navigate buses, trains, and subways is a rite of passage, offering a taste of independence and a lesson in logistics. Whether headed to school, work, or just out exploring, understanding how to use public transportation systems can make your travels smoother and more enjoyable.

Navigating Public Transit. Reading schedules and maps is the first step to becoming a savvy transit rider. Most transit systems have these available online, at stations, or through dedicated apps. Start by identifying your departure and arrival points on the system map. Look for the routes connecting these points and note any transfers you must make. Then, check the schedule for your route to find the times that work best for you. Remember, peak hours affect frequency and travel time, so plan accordingly.

For real-time information, many transit systems offer apps or text alert services that provide up-to-the-minute updates on schedules, delays, and even which bus or train car is less crowded. Taking advantage of these tools can save you time and reduce the stress of uncertainty.

Safety and Etiquette. Riding public transit is not just about getting from point A to point B; it's also about sharing space respectfully with others. Here are some tips to ensure a safe and pleasant journey for everyone:

- **Stay Alert:** Keep your belongings close, and be aware of your surroundings, especially in crowded or unfamiliar areas.

- **Offer Your Seat:** If you see someone who could use a seat more than you—like an older adult, a pregnant woman, or someone with a disability—offer yours up.

- **Keep the Noise Down:** Listen to music with headphones and keep phone conversations quiet and brief.

- **Make Space:** Backpacks can take up extra room and be cumbersome in tight spaces. Keep yours on your lap or between your feet.

Following these simple guidelines helps create a comfortable environment for all riders and fosters a culture of courtesy and respect.

Benefits of Public Transit. Choosing public transportation over a personal vehicle has several unique and global advantages. It's often more cost-effective, especially when you factor in expenses like gas, parking, and maintenance associated with car ownership. It also provides a perfect opportunity to catch up on reading, homework, or just some alone time with your thoughts—luxuries that driving doesn't afford.

On a larger scale, public transit plays a crucial role in reducing traffic congestion and lowering greenhouse gas emissions. Opting for buses or trains contributes to a cleaner, healthier environment and promotes sustainable urban development.

Alternative Transportation Options. Sometimes, public transit might align differently with your schedule or destination. In these cases, alternative transportation options can fill the gap:

- **Biking:** Many cities have invested in bike lanes and bike-sharing programs, making cycling a viable and eco-friendly option. Plus, it's great exercise!

- **Carpooling:** Sharing a ride with friends and family or through a carpool app can reduce costs and emissions. It's also a chance for social interaction and can make longer commutes more enjoyable.

- **Walking:** Don't underestimate the power of your own two feet for shorter distances. Walking is free, has zero environmental impact, and offers health benefits.

Each alternative has advantages and can be combined with public transit for a seamless transportation plan that fits your needs and lifestyle. In wrapping up, navigating public transportation and exploring alternative transportation options equips you with valuable life skills and connects you to the broader community and environment. By embracing these modes of travel, you're stepping into a world of independence and responsibility, all while contributing to a more sustainable future. As we move forward, remember that the choices you make in how you get around can have far-reaching effects on your personal development and the world around you.

Chapter Nine

Physical Health

P icture this: the sheer exhilaration of reaching the peak of a hill on your bike, the wind teasing your hair, a sense of achievement coursing through your veins. Or that content, glowing feeling after a long walk with friends, chatting and laughing as you explore new paths. Physical activity isn't just about sweat and numbers on a scale; it's about experiences, emotions, and the joy of moving your body in ways that make you feel alive. In this chapter, we dive into the diverse world of exercise tailored for you, setting achievable goals and reaping the benefits that extend far beyond the physical.

Diverse Exercise Options. The beauty of exercise lies in its variety. There's something out there for everyone, whether you're into the calm of yoga, the intensity of a HIIT session, or the thrill of skateboarding. Consider these options:

- **Team Sports** are great for those who thrive on camaraderie. Soccer, basketball, and volleyball are about physical fitness and building teamwork and social skills.

- **Solo Activities**: Would you prefer a solo venture? Running, swimming, or cycling could be your go-to. They offer flexibility, allowing you to set your own pace and schedule.

- **Dance**: Dance classes are perfect for music lovers and those who want to express themselves. From hip-hop to ballet, these classes mix creativity with exercise.

- **Martial Arts**: For discipline, self-defense, and fitness, martial arts like karate, judo, or boxing are excellent. They also boost confidence and concentration.

Finding an activity you enjoy is critical. It shouldn't feel like a chore but something you look forward to.

Setting Achievable Goals. Setting goals gives you direction and motivation. But remember, they should be realistic. Here's how you can set goals that keep you motivated without burning you out:

- Start small. If running a marathon is your dream, begin with a 5K.

- Be specific. Instead of "exercise more," aim for "jog 30 minutes thrice a week."

- Track progress. Celebrate small victories. Run a minute longer? That's a win.

- Adjust as needed. Goals aren't set in stone. Life happens, and it's okay to tweak your goals.

Benefits Beyond the Physical. Exercise does wonders for your body, but its impact on your mental and emotional well-being is just as profound:

- **Stress Relief**: Physical activity increases the production of endorphins, the body's natural mood lifters. It's like hitting a 'reset' button on your stress levels.

- **Improved Sleep**: Regular exercisers often report better sleep quality. Avoid vigorous activity close to bedtime, as it can have the opposite effect.

- **Boosted Confidence**: Achieving fitness goals, no matter how small, can significantly increase your self-esteem and body image.

Remember, the goal is to feel good, not just look good.

Incorporating Exercise into Daily Life. Fitting exercise into a busy schedule might seem challenging, but with a bit of creativity, it's entirely doable:

- **Walk or Bike**: Consider walking or biking to school or work. It's eco-friendly and provides your daily dose of activity.

- **Active Hangouts**: Next time you meet up with friends, suggest something active, such as a hike, a game of frisbee, or even a dance-off in your living room.

- **Short Bursts**: Got 10 minutes between homework assignments? Do a quick workout video or jump rope. It adds up.

- **Family Time**: Involve your family. Evening walks, weekend hikes, or yoga sessions at home can be great for bonding.

Embracing physical activity is about finding joy in movement and celebrating what your body can do. It's about setting realistic goals, acknowledging the mental and emotional perks, and weaving exercise into the fabric of your daily life. With the right approach, staying active becomes less about obligation and more about pleasure and well-being.

Nutrition Basics: Eating Well to Live Well. Feeding your body the proper nutrients is like fueling a car for a long trip; it requires quality fuel for optimal performance. In the bustling life of a teenager, understanding what your body needs to stay energized and healthy is crucial.

Understanding Nutritional Needs. Navigating through the maze of nutritional advice begins with grasping the basics. Your body craves a mix of essential nutrients to thrive:

- **Carbohydrates**: Often misconstrued as the enemy, carbohydrates are your body's primary energy source. For sustained energy, opt for whole grains, fruits, and vegetables over sugary snacks.

- **Proteins**: The building blocks of your muscles and organs. Lean meats, beans, and tofu are excellent sources.

- **Fats**: Not all fats are created equal. Unsaturated fats in avocados, nuts, and fish support brain health and energy.

- **Vitamins and Minerals**: These support various body

functions. A colorful plate ensures a variety of nutrients.

- **Water**: Often overlooked, staying hydrated is vital to maintaining energy levels and aiding digestion.

Understanding these elements leads to making informed choices about what to eat, ensuring your body gets what it needs to function at its best.

Making Healthy Food Choices. Selecting food that nourishes your body doesn't mean sacrificing flavor or enjoyment:

- **Listen to Your Body**: Eat when you're hungry and stop when you're full. Trusting your body's signals is fundamental.

- **Read Labels**: Not all packaged foods are off-limits. Understanding food labels can help you make healthier choices.

- **Variety is Key**: Aiming for a rainbow of colors on your plate ensures a wide range of nutrients.

- **Moderation, Not Deprivation**: It's okay to indulge occasionally. The goal is balance, allowing for treats without guilt.

Healthy eating is not about strict limitations or dietary fads. It's about enjoying food that tastes good and is suitable for you.

Meal Planning and Preparation. Finding time to eat healthily can be challenging with school, extracurricular activities, and social commitments. Here's how to make it manageable:

- **Plan Ahead**: Take time each week to plan meals and

snacks. This can save time and reduce stress on busy days.

- **Batch Cooking**: Prepare meals in bulk and store portions for later. This strategy is a lifesaver during hectic weeks.

- **Simple Recipes**: Meals don't have to be complicated. Simple dishes with a few healthy ingredients can be just as satisfying.

- **Involve Family or Friends**: Cooking with others can make meal prep more fun and less of a chore.

Meal planning and prep ensure that you have healthy options even on your busiest days.

Navigating Eating Out. Eating out is a part of life, and it doesn't have to derail your healthy eating habits:

- **Check the Menu Ahead**: Many restaurants offer their menus online. Look ahead and decide on a healthy option so cravings do not sway you.

- **Portion Control**: Restaurant servings can be generous. Consider sharing a dish or asking for a half portion.

- **Mindful Choices**: Choose grilled, baked, or steamed dishes rather than fried. And don't be shy about requesting substitutions, like a side salad instead of fries.

- **Balance Your Meal**: If you choose a less healthy main dish, balance it with healthier sides. Or, if you're eyeing dessert, start with a lighter main course.

Eating out doesn't mean you have to compromise on nutrition. With some foresight and balance, you can enjoy meals out without guilt. Nutrition isn't just about eating the right foods; it's about creating a relationship with positive and nourishing food. Whether cooking at home, planning meals for the week, or dining out, your choices can support your body's needs and taste preferences. Remember, healthy eating is a form of self-respect, giving your body the fuel it needs to achieve your dreams and tackle your goals.

Sleep Strategies: The Teen's Guide to Better Rest. Sleep, often overlooked in the hustle of daily routines and the glow of screens that command our attention plays a pivotal role in our well-being. During these quiet hours, our bodies repair, our brains consolidate memories, and our emotions find balance. Quality sleep is beneficial and crucial for teens navigating the complexities of growth and learning.

The Critical Role of Sleep. Sleep impacts nearly every aspect of our health. Physically, it's the time when the body repairs muscles, organs, and cells. Mentally, a good night's rest is intertwined with our ability to learn, focus, and retain information, directly influencing academic performance. Emotionally, adequate sleep helps regulate moods and stress levels, making challenges more manageable and joys more profound. Yet, the demands of school, social life, and extracurriculars, coupled with the allure of late-night entertainment and social media, often push sleep to the back burner.

Common Sleep Challenges. Several hurdles stand in the way of teens getting the rest they need. Irregular sleep schedules, a hallmark of teenage life, confuse our internal clocks, making it harder to fall asleep and wake up. The blue light emitted by screens can interfere with the production of melatonin, the hormone that signals our brain it's time to sleep, keeping us alert when we should be winding down. Anxiety and stress, whether from academic pressures or personal issues, can also control the mind racing long into the night.

Developing a Sleep Routine. A consistent sleep routine can do wonders for your rest. Here are some strategies to build one:

- **Set a Regular Bedtime and Wake Time**: Stick to these times as closely as possible, even on weekends. This consistency helps regulate your body's internal clock and improves the quality of your sleep.

- **Wind Down Before Bed**: Establish a pre-sleep ritual to signal your body to rest. This could be reading, listening to calming music, or practicing relaxation exercises.

- **Limit Naps**: While tempting, long or late-day naps can hinder nighttime sleep. If you must nap, aim for 20-30 minutes earlier in the afternoon.

Creating a Sleep-Conducive Environment. The environment in which you sleep can significantly affect how well you rest. Here are some aspects to consider:

- **Light**: Avoid exposure to bright lights in the evening. Keep your room dark with blackout curtains or a sleep mask.

- **Noise**: A quiet room is essential for undisturbed sleep. If you can't control external sounds, consider a white noise machine or earplugs.

- **Temperature**: Cooler temperatures are generally better for sleep. Aim to keep your room comfortably cool, around 65-68°F (18-20°C).

- **Comfort**: Invest in a good quality mattress and pillows that support your body comfortably.

In today's fast-paced world, where the night often feels too short for the day's tasks, prioritizing sleep is a declaration of self-care. It's about giving your body the rest it deserves to face each new day with energy, focus, and a balanced mind.

Understanding Substance Abuse: Making Informed Choices. Substance abuse is a topic often shrouded in myths and misconceptions, leading many teens down a path they initially believe they control. However, the reality is starkly different. Substance abuse can take a significant toll on every aspect of your life, from your physical health and mental state to your dreams and prospects. Recognizing the risks and knowing how to navigate these challenges is crucial.

Risks of Substance Abuse. The impact of substance abuse extends far beyond the momentary highs. Its repercussions can ripple through your life, affecting your body, mind, and future.

- **Physical Health**: Substance abuse can lead to a host of health issues, including heart problems, liver disease, respiratory distress, and a weakened immune system. When the body is still developing, the damage can be even more profound for those in their teen years.

- **Mental Well-being**: Beyond the physical toll, substances can wreak havoc on your mental health. They can exacerbate or trigger conditions like depression, anxiety, and psychosis. What might start as a way to cope can quickly become a factor that deepens mental health struggles.

- **Future Opportunities**: The choices made during your teen years can shape your future. Substance abuse can lead to academic struggles, loss of scholarships, difficulties in securing jobs, and legal issues—all of which can alter the course of your life.

Peer Pressure and Substance Use. One of the most significant factors in teen substance abuse is peer pressure. The desire to fit in or fear of being left out can push many into making choices they wouldn't otherwise consider. Here's how you can stand your ground:

- **Know Your Values**: Knowing what you stand for can help you navigate peer pressure. When you're firm in your beliefs, saying no becomes more accessible.

- **Choose Your Friends Wisely**: Surround yourself with friends who respect your choices and who you don't feel pressured to impress with risky behavior.

- **Have an Exit Strategy**: Sometimes, the best move is to walk away. Having a plan for exiting uncomfortable situations can save you from regretful choices.

- **Confidence in 'No'**: Saying no doesn't have to be confrontational. Practice ways to decline offers firmly but politely.

Seeking Help and Support. If you or someone you know is struggling with substance use, seeking help early can make a significant difference. Here's where you can turn:

- **Trusted Adults**: Whether it's a parent, teacher, or school counselor, find an adult you trust to talk about what you're going through.

- **Professional Help**: Therapists and counselors specializing in substance abuse can offer guidance and treatment plans tailored to your needs.

- **Support Groups**: Groups like Alateen provide a safe space to share experiences and learn from others facing similar challenges.

- **Hotlines**: Several hotlines offer anonymous, judgment-free support for those struggling with substance use.

The most important thing to remember is that asking for help is a sign of strength, not weakness.

Preventive Education. Education plays a pivotal role in preventing substance abuse. Understanding the facts, the risks, and the consequences can empower you to make informed decisions.

- **School Programs**: Engage in school-based programs that offer factual information about substances and their effects. These programs can debunk myths and provide a realistic picture of substance use.

- **Open Conversations**: Encourage open, honest discussions about substance use at home and with friends. Sharing knowledge and experiences can demystify substances and reduce their appeal.

- **Critical Thinking**: Learn to evaluate the information critically and influences around you, including media messages and peer stories. Only some things you hear or see are accurate.

Informed choices come from a place of knowledge and understanding. By educating yourself about the risks of substance abuse and developing strategies to resist peer pressure, you're setting a foundation for a healthier, more fulfilling life. Remember, your future is in your hands, and your decisions today will shape your world tomorrow.

Sexual Health: What Teens Need to Know. The topic of sexual health is often tiptoed around, shrouded in whispers and gossip. Yet, in the tapestry of adolescent life, understanding your sexual health and rights lays the groundwork for making empowered decisions about your body and relationships. It's about peeling away layers of myths to expose the facts, ensuring you're armed with knowledge that safeguards your well-being.

Accurate, Age-Appropriate Information. In the realm of sexual health, misinformation can spread faster than facts. A solid foundation in the basics — understanding your anatomy, the mechanics of reproduction, and the spectrum of gender and sexuality — is crucial. This knowledge empowers you to navigate your sexual health with confidence, recognizing normal development and when to seek medical advice.

- **Consent and Communication**: These are the bedrock of all healthy relationships. Knowing that consent is a clear, enthusiastic, and ongoing agreement between all parties involved in any sexual activity is vital. Equally important is the ability to communicate your boundaries and respect those of others.

- **Contraception and STI Prevention**: Understanding the various forms of contraception, their use, and effectiveness protects against unintended pregnancies and sexually transmitted infections (STIs). Equally, knowing the signs of STIs and the importance of regular testing can prevent long-term health issues.

Navigating Relationships and Consent. The dynamics of relationships and the concept of consent are evolving. Recognizing and respecting personal boundaries and clear communication are crucial to fostering positive and healthy interactions.

- **Healthy Relationships**: These are built on mutual respect, trust, and honesty. Identifying signs of healthy versus unhealthy relationships helps you make informed choices about who you associate with intimately.

- **The Role of Consent**: It's about saying yes or no freely without pressure or coercion. It's dynamic, meaning it can be withdrawn at any time, and it must be obtained before every sexual activity.

Accessing Resources and Support. Knowing where and how to access sexual health services provides a safety net for confidential advice, testing, and treatment.

- **Confidential Services**: Many clinics offer confidential sexual health services to teens, including contraception advice, STI testing, and counseling. Familiarizing yourself with these services ensures you know where to turn when in need.

- **Online Resources**: Reliable online platforms provide a wealth of information on sexual health. However, it is crucial to discern credible sources from misinformation.

Debunking Myths and Misconceptions. The myths surrounding sexual health are many, and believing them can lead to anxiety, misinformed decisions, and health risks.

- **Myth vs. Fact**: For instance, the belief that STIs can only be contracted through full sexual intercourse is false. Understanding the ways STIs can be transmitted helps in taking appropriate preventive measures.

- **The Impact of Pornography**: Pornography often presents a distorted view of sex, which can impact expectations and understanding of healthy sexual relationships. Recognizing this can help in forming realistic opinions about sex and intimacy.

In navigating the waters of adolescence, where you're discovering and asserting your identity, understanding your sexual health is vital. It's not just about protecting yourself from risks but also about building respectful, fulfilling relationships. This knowledge acts as a compass, guiding you through choices that honor your well-being and values.

As we close this exploration, it's clear that sexual health is an integral part of your overall well-being. The courage to seek out facts, communicate openly, and respect personal boundaries lays a strong foundation for a healthy, informed, and respectful approach to relationships and sexuality. Armed with accurate information and support networks, you're better prepared to navigate the complexities of sexual health and relationships, making choices that align with your values and well-being.

Moving forward, the journey into understanding and taking charge of your health and relationships continues. Each step, armed with knowledge and compassion, brings you closer to embracing a life of informed choices, well-being, and respect for yourself and others.

Building and Nurturing Friendships

I magine walking into a room full of strangers. Your palms are sweaty, your heart races, and your thoughts race. Now, reimagine that scenario, but this time, among those strangers, you spot a familiar face, someone you share a bond with. Suddenly, the room doesn't feel so daunting anymore. This shift highlights the power of friendships as social connections and anchors in our ever-changing lives. Navigating high school and beyond comes with its set of challenges. Still, with the right approach to building and nurturing friendships, you can turn these experiences into opportunities for growth and connection.

Making New Friends: Tips for High School and Beyond

Openness to New Experiences. Life is a mosaic of experiences, each piece colored by the people we meet along the way. High schools, clubs, sports, and online communities are bustling hubs where friendships can bloom. Picture yourself signing up for a photography club or joining a local soccer team; these are not just activities but doorways to meeting people with similar interests. The key? Keep an open mind. Attend that meet-up, participate in community events, or hit that 'Join' button on an online forum you've been eyeing. New experiences are the soil in which new friendships grow.

Common Interests. Imagine finding someone who laughs at the same obscure TV show jokes as you or is equally excited about environmental conservation. Shared interests are the glue that binds people together. High school and community clubs are treasure troves of shared interest groups. Whether it's the drama club, the science team, or a local gaming group, these settings provide a common ground from which conversations flow more freely and connections deepen.

First Impressions. They say you never get a second chance to make a first impression. When meeting new people, how you present yourself can set the tone for future interactions. But re-member, being genuine trumps everything. Wear that smile, offer a friendly greeting, and let your personality shine. Authenticity attracts, and being true to yourself will draw others who appreciate you for who you are.

Initiating Conversations. Starting a conversation can feel like standing at the edge of a diving board. The key is to leap. Ask open-ended questions that invite others to share about themselves. "What's your favorite part about being in the club?" or "How did you get interested in this sport?" are gateways to more profound dialogues. Listen actively and show genuine interest, and the con-versation will flow. Remember, everyone has a story waiting to be told, and showing interest in theirs can begin a beautiful friendship.

Healthy vs. Toxic Relationships: Recognizing the Signs. In the garden of life, friendships are the flowers that add color, fragrance, and joy. Like all living things, these relationships need the right conditions to thrive. Understanding what nurtures friendship and what poisons it is crucial for anyone navigating the complex web of high school social life and beyond.

Characteristics of Healthy Friendships. In a world bustling with diverse personalities, a tapestry of healthy friendships can be woven with threads of:

- **Mutual Respect**: Each person values the other's feelings, thoughts, and boundaries, celebrating differences rather than allowing them to divide.

- **Support**: True friends are the pillars you can lean on during storms and the cheerleaders in your moments of triumph. They're there for you, offering a listening ear, a shoulder to cry on, or a high five when you succeed.

- **Honesty**: Honesty is the foundation of trust in any friendship. It's about truthful and open communication, where individuals feel safe sharing their thoughts and feelings.

These elements create a nurturing environment where friendships can flourish, promoting growth and happiness for everyone involved.

Warning Signs of Toxic Relationships. However, not all relationships contribute positively to our lives. Some might start well but turn toxic, while others are unhealthy. Recognizing these red flags can help you steer clear of emotional harm:

- **Manipulation**: If a friend frequently tries to control your actions or decisions, often through guilt or pressure, it's a sign of manipulation.

- **Disrespect** can manifest as belittling comments, disregard for your boundaries, or a consistent lack of consideration for your feelings and needs.

- **One-sidedness**: A friendship should be a two-way street. If you find that you're always giving—be it time, attention, or support—with little to nothing in return, it's time to reassess the balance in your relationship.

- **Constant Drama**: Disagreements are expected if a friendship is consistently filled with conflict, gossip, or negativity; it might do more harm than good.

Setting Boundaries. Healthy boundaries are like garden fences; they protect and define. Here's how to establish them effectively.

- **Identify Your Limits**: Spend some time reflecting on what you're comfortable with in a friendship. What are your deal-breakers? What do you need to feel respected and supported?

- **Communicate Clearly**: Once you know your boundaries, express them to your friends in clear, assertive language. It's not about making demands but sharing what you need to feel happy and safe in the relationship.

- **Be Consistent**: Enforcing boundaries isn't a one-time thing. You may need to remind friends of your limits occasionally, and that's okay.

Seeking Help. Sometimes, despite our best efforts, we find ourselves entangled in toxic friendships that we're unsure how to escape. If you're feeling trapped, overwhelmed, or scared, it's essential to seek help:

- **Talk to Someone You Trust**: This could be a parent, another friend, a teacher, or a school counselor. They can offer advice, support, and perspective on the situation.

- **Professional Support**: If a toxic friendship is significantly impacting your mental health, consider speaking with a therapist. They can provide strategies for handling the relationship and healing from any emotional damage.

Remember, removing yourself from a toxic friendship isn't a failure. It's a brave step towards prioritizing your well-being and making room for healthier, more fulfilling connections.

Dealing with Loneliness and Isolation. Loneliness often creeps up silently, like shadows lengthening as the day draws closer. It's a feeling that can envelop anyone, even amidst a crowd or in the bustling hallways of high school. Feeling isolated or disconnected impacts not only our mental health but seeps into our daily functioning, clouding our perceptions and experiences with a tinge of sadness.

Understanding Loneliness. At its core, loneliness is an emotional response to a perceived lack of connection and companionship. It's essential to recognize that feeling this way is normal, especially during change or transition. With their rapid developments and shifts, the teenage years are prime grounds for such feelings to surface. Acknowledging loneliness as a shared experience can be the first step in addressing its hold on our lives.

Healthy Coping Mechanisms

- **Stay Active**: Engage in physical activities or hobbies that you enjoy. Whether it's a solo jog in the park, painting, or playing an instrument, these activities can offer solace and a sense of achievement.

- **Mindfulness and Meditation**: Practicing mindfulness or meditation can help ground you in the present moment and offer a break from the cycle of loneliness-inducing thoughts.

- **Journaling**: Writing down your thoughts and feelings can provide an outlet for expression and self-reflection. It's a way to process emotions and clarify why you might feel lonely.

These coping mechanisms offer a way to navigate through feelings of loneliness, providing a sense of control and empowerment over our emotional state.

Reaching Out. Often, the thought of reaching out can seem daunting, overshadowed by the fear of rejection or the belief that others won't understand. Yet, opening up to someone, be it a friend, family member, or counselor, can be incredibly freeing. It's a reminder that you don't have to face these feelings alone. Conversation can be a bridge, reconnecting us with those around us and reinforcing the support networks we might have overlooked.

- **Start Small**: If opening up feels overwhelming, start with small, manageable conversations. It doesn't have to be about loneliness initially; engaging in dialogue can gradually build your comfort level.

- **Choose the Right Person**: Think about someone in your life who is empathetic and a good listener. This person should be someone you trust and feel comfortable with.

- **Be Honest**: When you're ready, be honest about what you're experiencing. Honesty paves the way for genuine connection and support.

Finding Community. Finding a community can be a beacon of hope to combat loneliness. Communities, whether based on shared interests, experiences, or goals, offer a sense of belonging and understanding that can be hard to find elsewhere.

- **Explore Local Clubs or Groups**: Many communities have clubs or groups centered around hobbies, sports, or volunteering. These can be great ways to meet new people who share your interests.

- **Online Forums and Social Media**: The digital world is vast, with countless forums, groups, and platforms where individuals can connect over shared experiences or interests. Whether it's a forum dedicated to a particular hobby or a social media group for local volunteers, the internet can bridge geographical gaps and connect you with a global community.

- **Attend Meetups or Events**: Look for local events or meetups related to your interests. These can be excellent opportunities to engage with others in a relaxed, social setting.

Finding and engaging with a community alleviates loneliness and enriches our lives with diverse interactions and friendships. It's about taking that small step towards connecting with others and rediscovering the joy of shared experiences.

In navigating through loneliness and isolation, it's crucial to remember that these feelings don't define us. They're a part of the human experience, a reminder of our need for connection and companionship. We can move through these feelings by understanding loneliness, employing healthy coping mechanisms, reaching out for support, and finding our community. Each step taken is a stride towards a more connected and fulfilled self that recognizes the value of relationships and the strength of togetherness.

Communicating Effectively with Friends: The Key to Lasting Relationships. In the tapestry of friendships, the threads of communication weave patterns of understanding, trust, and mutual respect. How we talk and listen to each other paints the picture of our relationships, highlighting the importance of effective communication as the cornerstone of lasting bonds.

Active Listening. Imagine a scenario where a friend shares a personal story, but instead of genuinely listening, you're mentally rehearsing your response or thinking about something else entirely. This moment, ripe for connection, can easily slip away. Active listening fully engages with the speaker, absorbing their words, emotions, and the unspoken nuances of their message. It's about making eye contact, nodding in acknowledgment, and offering feedback that shows you're not just hearing but understanding. When friends feel listened to, it deepens the bond, creating a safe space where openness flourishes.

- **Echo their sentiments**: Paraphrase or summarize what your friend has said to show you're paying attention.

- **Ask open-ended questions**: Encourage them to share more by asking questions that require more than a yes or no answer.

- **Avoid interrupting**: Let them express their thoughts fully before you respond.

Expressing Needs and Feelings. Friendships thrive on honesty and vulnerability, yet expressing our deepest needs and feelings can sometimes feel like navigating a minefield. The fear of being misunderstood or rejected might hold you back. However, sharing what's on your mind and heart is vital for building trust and intimacy. Use "I" statements to frame your feelings and needs without placing blame. For instance, "I feel overlooked when we don't spend time together" is more constructive than "You never make time for me." This approach opens the door to understanding without triggering defensiveness.

- **Be clear and specific**: Vagueness can lead to misunderstandings. Be specific about what you're feeling and why.

- **Choose the right time and place**: Important conversations require a calm environment where both parties feel comfortable and undistracted.

- **Practice empathy**: Consider how your friend might receive your words, and approach sensitive topics with care and respect.

Conflict Resolution. Disagreements and misunderstandings are inevitable in any relationship. Yet, it's not the conflict itself but how we handle it, that defines the strength of a friendship. Approaching disagreements to find a solution rather than winning an argument can transform conflicts into opportunities for growth. Start by calmly stating your perspective and then genuinely listen to theirs. Look for common ground or areas of compromise. Sometimes, agreeing to disagree while respecting each other's viewpoints can be the most harmonious outcome.

- **Stay focused on the issue**: Avoid bringing up past grievances.

- **Use non-accusatory language**: Focus on how the situation makes you feel rather than blaming the other person.

- **Seek solutions together**: Collaborate on finding a resolution that satisfies both parties.

Maintaining Connections. As time unfolds, life can lead friends in different directions. Physical distance, busy schedules, and life changes can strain even the strongest bonds. Keeping the flame of friendship alive requires intentional effort.

- **Regular check-ins**: A simple message or call to say "thinking of you" can make all the difference.

- **Schedule time together**: Plan regular meet-ups, whether in person or virtual and stick to them as you would any critical commitment.

- **Celebrate essential moments**: Remember birthdays, achievements, and milestones, and reach out to share in their joy.

- **Be adaptable**: Understand how your connection might change over time. What matters is keeping the lines of communication open, whether through text, calls, social media, or letters.

In friendships, effective communication is the magic that turns ordinary connections into enduring relationships. It's about listening with empathy, sharing openly and honestly, navigating conflicts with care, and staying connected despite life's inevitable changes. Through these practices, friendships can grow more profound, meaningful, and resilient, enriching our lives with the joy and support only true friends can provide.

Navigating Friendships and Romantic Relationships. Friendships and romantic interests often run on parallel tracks, sometimes intersecting in ways that add complexity to our lives. Striking a balance between these relationships is not just about dividing your calendar but also about sharing your emotional world.

When love enters the scene, it brings a whirlwind of emotions and changes that can affect friendships, sometimes unexpectedly.

Navigating these waters requires a thoughtful approach, ensuring that while new relationships bloom, old ones don't wither. It's about recognizing that each relationship, whether platonic or romantic, plays a unique role in our lives and contributes to our growth and happiness.

Balancing Friendships and Romantic Interests. Imagine your week as a pie chart, with slices allocated to different activities and people. When a romantic interest comes into the picture, giving them the lion's share is tempting, but balance is critical. Here are some tips for maintaining equilibrium:

- **Prioritize Quality Time**: Make an effort to spend quality time with friends and your romantic partner, ensuring each feels valued.

- **Communicate Openly**: Talk to your friends and partner about your need to maintain both relationships. Often, simply knowing you're mindful of their feelings can ease potential tensions.

- **Flexible Scheduling**: Be creative with your time. Group activities can be fun, such as merging friend groups with your partner and fostering new connections.

Navigating New Dynamics. When friends start dating within the same circle, the dynamic inevitably shifts. Suddenly, there are new sensitivities to navigate, and the existing balance may feel off-kilter. Here's how to adapt:

- **Embrace Change**: Accept that relationships evolve, and

with them, friendships can too. This doesn't mean losing depth; sometimes, it means growing together differently.

- **Support Your Friends**: Support your friends' new relationships, showing genuine interest and happiness.

- **Create New Traditions**: As dynamics shift, old traditions may not fit as well. Be proactive in creating new ones that include everyone.

Respecting Boundaries. In all relationships, boundaries are essential. They define where one person ends and the other begins, creating a safe space for individuals to thrive. Here are ways to respect boundaries:

- **Understand Limits**: Every relationship has different boundaries. Take the time to understand what's comfortable for each person, including yourself.

- **Communicate**: If you're unsure about a boundary, ask. It's better to have a conversation than to overstep unintentionally.

- **Respect Privacy**: Both friends and romantic partners deserve privacy. Avoid the urge to snoop or press for information they're not ready to share.

Communication in Relationships. At the heart of any strong relationship is communication. The thread ties understanding, trust, and respect together, creating a bond that can withstand challenges. In romantic relationships, this becomes even more critical.

- **Honest Conversations**: Be honest about your feelings, hopes, and fears. Encouraging your partner to do the same can deepen your connection.

- **Listen Actively**: Show that you value your partner's thoughts by listening attentively, validating their feelings, and responding thoughtfully.

- **Resolve Conflicts Constructively**: Approach disagreements to resolve rather than win. Focus on understanding each other's perspectives and finding a middle ground.

Navigating the intricate dance between friendships and romantic relationships is an ongoing process. It's about giving each the attention and care it deserves without sacrificing one for the other. This delicate balance enriches our lives, offering a spectrum of experiences and emotions that contribute to our personal growth.

In wrapping up, we've explored the dynamics of maintaining friendships while managing romantic relationships. The essence lies in balance, open communication, respect for boundaries, and adapting to changing dynamics. These principles ensure the health of our connections and contribute to our growth as individuals.

As we move forward, let's carry these insights into our broader social interactions, recognizing the value of every connection we make. In the next chapter, we delve into facing social challenges, equipping you with the skills to navigate the complexities of social situations with confidence and grace.

Conclusion

A s we draw the curtains on this enlightening journey, I am compelled to reflect on the ground we've covered together. We embarked on this voyage with a simple mission: to better understand ourselves and navigate the ever-evolving digital landscapes that mark our era. We ventured through the pillars of financial independence, embraced the essence of practical life skills, and took a deep dive into physical and mental well-being. Our path was intertwined with exploring the intricacies of complex social relationships, each step revealing a new layer of understanding and self-discovery.

The core life skills we've delved into—effective communication, emotional intelligence, financial literacy, digital safety, stress management, and building healthy relationships—are not just individual tools. They are interconnected strands that, woven together, form the fabric of a well-rounded, confident, and capable adult.

Each skill is a thread in the tapestry of life, where mastering one area can spark growth in another, creating a domino effect of personal development and resilience.

This book was envisioned as a beacon to illuminate the path for teens navigating the murky waters of transition. The unique pressures of today's world are formidable, but they are navigable with the right compass. We aimed to provide insights and actionable advice—strategies that leap off the page and into your life, exercises that challenge you, scenarios that reflect your experiences, and practical tips that encourage you to apply what you've learned.

I urge you to practice these skills actively. Embrace the journey with all its ups and downs, for mastery is a continual process that demands patience, practice, and perseverance. Remember, setbacks are not failures but stepping stones to growth. The skills outlined in these pages are your arsenal in facing the challenges ahead.

But don't let your exploration end here. I encourage you to seek further knowledge, engage in new experiences, and keep the lines of communication open with peers, parents, and mentors. Your support systems are invaluable allies in this quest. Lean on them, learn from them, and let them guide you as you apply these skills in the real world.

Looking towards the horizon, I am filled with hope and excitement for your future. Armed with these life skills, you stand on the threshold of adulthood, ready to face its challenges, make informed choices, and lead a fulfilling life. Approach the future with optimism, with the knowledge, readiness, and confidence to carve your path and make your mark on the world.

Thank you for joining me on this journey. I hope this book serves as a guide and a companion on your path to becoming the best version of yourself. Here's to your growing-up journey—a journey filled with learning, growth, and endless possibilities.

With gratitude and best wishes for your future,

Robert James Ryan

If you're navigating the challenges of raising children in today's fast-paced world, you understand the importance of giving them the right start. This book could make a significant impact on their daily lives, and I would be deeply honored if you chose to purchase it by clicking **"Buy Now With 1-Click"** above. If even a few chapters can assist them, it's a worthwhile investment.

After reading, please consider leaving an honest review on the Amazon page. Every review counts more than you might think, helping the book rank higher and become more visible to others who could benefit from it.

Thank you immensely for considering this book. I truly hope it supports your child in overcoming their daily challenges. Simply scroll up, click **"Buy Now With 1-Click,"** and start their reading journey today!

References

References

Tips for Teens: Building Healthy Communication Skills
https://www.thrivetrainingconsulting.com/tips-for-teens-building-healthy-communication-skills

How Using Social Media Affects Teenagers - Child Mind Institute
https://childmind.org/article/how-using-social-media-affects-teenagers/

Peer Pressure: Strategies to Help Teens Handle it Effectively
https://parentandteen.com/handle-peer-pressure/

Teaching Active Listening Skills to High School Students
https://everydayspeech.com/blog-posts/general/teaching-active-listening-skills-to-high-school-students/

Mindfulness Exercises (for Teens) - Nemours KidsHealth
https://kidshealth.org/en/teens/mindful-exercises.html

How Using Social Media Affects Teenagers
https://childmind.org/article/how-using-social-media-affects-teenagers/

5 Strategies for Teaching Empathy to Teens

https://www.connectionsacademy.com/support/resources/article/teaching-empathy-to-teens

27 Resilience Activities for Students and Adults (+PDF)

https://positivepsychology.com/resilience-activities-worksheets/

Family Guide to Teaching Kids and Teens Essential Digital Skills

https://digitalwellnesslab.org/family-guides/empowering-digital-natives-a-guide-to-teaching-kids-and-teens-essential-digital-skills

Social Media's Concerning Effect on Teen Mental Health

https://www.aecf.org/blog/social-medias-concerning-effect-on-teen-mental-health

Cyberbullying: What is it and how to stop it - UNICEF

https://www.unicef.org/end-violence/how-to-stop-cyberbullying#:~:text=If%20the%20bullying%20is%20happening,and%20reporting%20it%20is%20key.

What Every Teen Needs to Know About Their Digital footprint...

https://www.netnanny.com/blog/what-every-teen-needs-to-know-about-their-digital-footprint/

Top 10 Apps to Enhance High School Students' Success

https://moonpreneur.com/blog/best-app-for-high-school-students

13 Time Management Techniques for Teens

https://student-tutor.com/blog/time-management-techniques-for-teens/

Advice to create a positive online reputation for kids:

https://www.internetmatters.org/issues/online-reputation/protect-your-child/

Introduction To Digital Art

https://www.udemy.com/course/introduction-to-digital-art/

23 Best Money Apps for Teens

https://www.kidsmoney.org/teens/money-management/apps/

How Your Credit Score Impacts Your Financial Future

https://www.finra.org/investors/personal-finance/how-your-credit-score-impacts-your-financial-future

14 Teen Entrepreneurs and How They Succeeded

https://www.oxford-royale.com/articles/14-teen-entrepreneurs/

The Student's Guide to College Loans

https://www.bestcolleges.com/resources/college-loans/

50 Cheap, Healthy Meals You'll Want to Make All the Time

https://www.tasteofhome.com/collection/cheap-healthy-meals/

How to Learn DIY Home Repair Skills for Free:

https://www.thepennyhoarder.com/save-money/diy-home-repair-skills-free/

8 Time Management Tips for Students - Harvard Summer School /

https://summer.harvard.edu/blog/8-time-management-tips-for-students

Tips for teens to stay safe on public transport:

https://nhw.com.au/children/tips-for-teens-to-stay-safe-on-public-transport/

Exercise for Teenagers: A Complete Guide

https://www.healthline.com/health/fitness/exercise-for-tee
nagers

Associations between Sleep and Mental Health in ...
https://www.ncbi.nlm.nih.gov/pmc/articles/PMC8835146/
Prevention, early intervention, and harm reduction of ...
https://www.ncbi.nlm.nih.gov/pmc/articles/PMC5418996
Data and Statistics on Children's Mental Health https://w
ww.cdc.gov/childrensmentalhealth/data.html

https://www.cdc.gov/childrensmentalhealth/data.html
Mindfulness Exercises (for Teens) - Nemours KidsHealth
https://kidshealth.org/en/teens/mindful-exercises.html
Teens need a strong and extensive support system. Here's ...
https://www.washingtonpost.com/lifestyle/2018/11/30/te
ens-need-strong-large-support-system-heres-how-help-them-b
uild-it/

Peer Pressure: Strategies to Help Teens Handle it Effectively
https://parentandteen.com/handle-peer-pressure/
17 Ways to Make New Friends in High School
https://www.wikihow.com/Make-New-Friends-in-High-Sc
hool

Toxic Friendship: 24 Signs, Effects, and Tips - Healthline
https://www.healthline.com/health/toxic-friendships
How To Cope With Loneliness As A Teenager
https://www.healthyyoungminds.com/how-to-cope-with-l
oneliness-as-a-teenager/#:~:text=Key%20Strategies%20to%20
Overcome%20Teenage,of%20self%2Dexpression%20and%20c
onnection.

Tips for Teens: Building Healthy Communication Skills

https://www.thrivetrainingconsulting.com/tips-for-teens-buil
ding-healthy-communication-skills

Evidence-Based Bullying Prevention Programs | CDE
https://www.cde.state.co.us/mtss/bullyingpreventionprogram
s

Peer Pressure: Strategies to Help Teens Handle it Effectively
https://parentandteen.com/handle-peer-pressure

Teens, Technology and Friendships
https://www.pewresearch.org/internet/2015/08/06/teens-tec
hnology-and-friendships/

How to Deal with Friendships Changing After High School
https://www.georgefox.edu/bruin-blog/posts/2021/01/changi
ng-friendships/index.htm

A.I was utilized in portions of this book

Printed in Great Britain
by Amazon